CONTEMPORARY COLOR DESIGN

daab

Architects/Designers	**Project**	

Architects/Designers	Project	

INTRODUCTION

Color in architecture is a hot topic. After a long phase in which straightforwardness and rationality set the tone for design and material colors at best complemented the look of white, black, and gray, many architects have been increasingly turning to the world of colors.

There appears to be no limit to the wealth of ideas, creativity, and selection of color. The projects presented here document very different perceptions and approaches: from the translation of the company colors as an expression of corporate identity in architecture to the sensitively developed concepts concerned with the effects that color has on the users and the surroundings. The effects of color and the reaction to it are subjective; for this reason alone, the selection of color by architects for their buildings is diverse and does not always follow the strict laws. Yet, there are general correspondences in the perception that the planners also agree upon.

Yellow—as the color of the sun and of light—is valued because of its brilliance. It has a bright and friendly effect in rooms. Yellow radiates the zest for life—and, most importantly, promotes communication. This makes it the appropriate ambience for a cocktail and food bar like the Nama in Stuttgart.

Red is the color of warmth and, above all, love. But blood is red as well. Fire and battle are also connected with this color, which warns against danger as signal red. The red theater in Lelystadt, as the heart of the building, radiates the warmth of this color. Its model is the setting evening sun above the Dutch city of Ijsselmeer. On the other hand, Dock 47—the dominant office building between the nightclub district and the Hamburg harbor—towers vehemently over the street area in signal red.

Blue creates associations with expansiveness—such as the ocean and the sky. It is a clear color that represents the intellect and the mind. As a result, the blue of the tiled school in Heilbronn stands for more than just the architect's favorite color. It is a symbol of learning. At White Blue Black in Tokyo—a residential building for book lovers—the collected knowledge rests exclusively on blue shelves.

Green is nature, the basis for our lives, which is restful as a color. Green stands between cool blue and warm yellow; it harmonizes and balances. It appears very natural to have educational institutions painted in this balancing color: the increase of knowledge and life experience as a natural growth process. However, the architects of the underground parking garage on the bank of the Rhine River in Mainz transport the meadow into a concrete-gray underworld. For the arriving drivers, the green creates anticipation for what is waiting for them on the bank of the Rhine.

The concepts of the architects presented here extend far beyond just painting the walls in a certain color. The materials and colors complement and communicate with each other. They open a new perspective of the interior and exterior for the observers: A historic monastery garden shimmers through the organza curtains and immerses a modern temple of consumerism in greenish light. Rough concrete formwork panels receive a yellow coat of paint and suddenly appear to be an identity-giving band between the cocktail bar and the snack bar. Birch trunks in their characteristic black-and-white serve as a semi-transparent room divider and give the surroundings a natural flair. A fire-red carpet turns out to be a soft floor covering of rubber granulate and transforms a gray plaza into a municipal living room.

Contemporary Color Design—literally—presents a colorful mixture of international architects and their projects: self-confidant statements, stimulating food for thought, uninhibited experiments, concepts that are humorous and full of life, as well as reserved approaches that are effective and set specific color accents.

Farbe in der Architektur ist ein aktuelles Thema. Nach einer langen Phase, in der Geradlinigkeit und Rationalität das Design prägten und allenfalls Materialfarben das Bild von Weiß, Schwarz und Grau ergänzten, wenden sich seit einiger Zeit viele Architekten verstärkt der Welt der Farben zu.

Dem Ideenreichtum, der Kreativität und der Farbwahl scheinen keine Grenzen gesetzt zu sein. Die vorgestellten Projekte dokumentieren sehr unterschiedliche Auffassungen und Vorgehensweisen: von der Übertragung der Unternehmensfarben als Ausdruck der Corporate Identity in die Architektur bis hin zu sensibel ausgearbeiteten Konzepten, die sich mit der Frage beschäftigen, wie Farbe auf den Nutzer und die Umgebung wirkt. Farbwirkung und Farbempfinden sind subjektiv; schon aus diesem Grund ist die Farbwahl der Architekten für ihre Gebäude vielfältig und folgt nicht immer strikten Gesetzmäßigkeiten. Dennoch gibt es allgemeingültige Übereinstimmungen in der Wahrnehmung, die auch die Planer aufgreifen.

Gelb, als Farbe der Sonne und des Lichtes, wird wegen seiner Leuchtkraft geschätzt. Räume wirken hell und freundlich. Gelb strahlt Lebensfreude aus – und fördert vor allem die Kommunikation. Das passende Ambiente also für eine Cocktail- und Foodbar wie die Nama in Stuttgart.
Rot ist die Farbe der Wärme und vor allem der Liebe. Aber auch das Blut ist rot. Feuer und der Kampf sind mit dieser Farbe verbunden, die als Signalrot vor Gefahr warnt. Der rote Theatersaal in Lelystadt, als Herz des Gebäudes, strahlt die Wärme dieser Farbe aus. Vorbild ist die untergehende Abendsonne über der niederländischen Stadt am Ijsselmeer. Dock 47, das dominante Bürogebäude zwischen Amüsierviertel und Hamburger Hafen, stemmt sich hingegen in signalrot kräftig in den Straßenraum.
Blau ruft Assoziationen von Weite hervor – wie das Meer und der Himmel. Es ist eine klare Farbe, die für den Verstand und für den Geist steht. Das Blau der gefliesten Schule in Heilbronn stellt somit mehr dar als nur die Lieblingsfarbe des Architekten. Sie ist Symbol für das Lernen. Im White Blue Black in Tokio, einem Wohnhaus für Buchliebhaber, ruht das gesammelte Wissen allein auf blauen Regalen.
Grün ist die Natur, unsere Lebensgrundlage, die als Farbe erholsam wirkt. Grün steht zwischen dem kühlen Blau und dem warmen Gelb; es harmonisiert und gleicht aus. Ganz natürlich scheint es zu sein, dass Bildungseinrichtungen in dieser ausgleichenden Farbe gehalten sind: Das Zunehmen des Wissens und der Lebenserfahrung als natür-

licher Wachstumsprozess. Die Architekten der Rheinufer-Tiefgarage in Mainz hingegen holen die Wiese in eine betongraue Unterwelt. Grün bereitet den ankommenden Autofahrern Vorfreude auf das, was sie am Rheinufer erwartet.

Die Konzepte der vorgestellten Architekten gehen weit über den bloßen farbigen Wandanstrich hinaus. Materialien und Farbe ergänzen sich und kommunizieren miteinander. Sie eröffnen den Betrachtern einen neuen Blick auf das Außen und das Innen: Ein historischer Klostergarten schimmert durch Organza-Vorhänge und taucht einen modernen Konsumtempel in grünliches Licht. Rohe Betonschaltafeln erhalten einen gelben Anstrich und wirken plötzlich wie ein identitätsstiftendes Band zwischen Cocktail- und Snackbar. Birkenstämme in ihrem charakteristischen Schwarz-Weiß dienen als semitransparenter Raumteiler und verleihen der Umgebung ein natürliches Flair. Ein feuerroter Teppich entpuppt sich als weicher Bodenbelag aus Gummigranulat und macht aus einem grauen Vorplatz ein städtisches Wohnzimmer.

Contemporary Color Design stellt eine – im wörtlichen Sinne – bunte Mischung internationaler Architekten und ihrer Projekte vor: selbstbewusste Statements, anregende Denkanstöße, unbefangene Experimente, humorvolle und lebensfrohe Auffassungen sowie zurückhaltende Annäherungen, die wirkungsvolle und gezielte Farbakzente setzen.

El color en la arquitectura es un tema muy en boga. Tras una larga etapa en la que los trazos rectos y la racionalidad han marcado el diseño y que, con mucho, los colores de los materiales eran un mero complemento al blanco, negro y gris, son muchos los arquitectos que desde hace un tiempo están dirigiendo sus miradas al mundo de los colores.

La imaginación, la creatividad y la elección de colores parecen no tener límites. Los proyectos aquí presentados documentan las concepciones y las formas de actuar más diversas: de la utilización de los colores de una empresa como expresión de la identidad corporativa en arquitectura a unos conceptos elaborados con mucha sensibilidad y que han intentado dar respuesta a la cuestión de la influencia de los colores tanto en el usuario como en el entorno. La influencia y la interpretación de los colores son subjetivas; por este motivo, las posibilidades de elección de colores por parte de los arquitectos son muchas y no siempre siguen una normativa estricta. No obstante, existe un convenio de aceptación general en cuanto a su apreciación, convenio al que también se adhieren los proyectistas.

El amarillo es el color del sol y de la luz. Es apreciado por su poder lumínico. Las estancias resultan luminosas y acogedoras. El amarillo irradia alegría de vivir y fomenta la comunicación. El ambiente adecuado para un restaurante y bar de copas como el Nama en la ciudad alemana de Stuttgart.
El rojo es el color del calor y especialmente del amor. Pero también la sangre es de este color. Fuego y lucha se asocian al rojo, color que también indica peligro. La sala del teatro de Lelystad, el corazón del edificio, irradia ese calor. Al caer la tarde, es digna de ver la puesta de sol en esta ciudad holandesa a orillas del lago Ijseel. El Dock 47, el imponente edificio rojo de oficinas situado entre el barrio chino y el puerto de Hamburgo, se alza con fuerza en medio del espacio urbano.
El azul se asocia con algo lejano, como puede ser el mar o el cielo. Es un color claro que representa la razón y el alma. El azul del instituto alicatado de la ciudad alemana de Heilbronn representa mucho más que el color preferido de los arquitectos. Simboliza el aprendizaje. En la White Blue Black de Tokio, una vivienda para un amante de los libros, todo el conocimiento acumulado descansa en estanterías azules.
El verde es naturaleza, la base de nuestra existencia. Es un color relajante. El verde se ubica entre el frío del azul y el calor del amarillo. Armoniza y equilibra. Parece pues de lo más lógico que los centros de enseñanza sean de este color, pues se representa así el aumento del conocimiento y la experiencia como un proceso natural de crecimiento. Los arquitectos del Garaje de la Ribera del Rin en la ciudad alemana de Maguncia llevan los prados a un mundo subterráneo dominado por el gris del hormigón. El verde prepara a los conductores para lo que les espera junto al Rin.

Los conceptos de estos arquitectos van más allá de lo que sería sencillamente pintar de un color una pared. Materiales y colores se complementan y se comunican entre sí. Le proporcionan al observador una nueva mirada por fuera y por dentro. Los brillos del jardín de un convento se filtran a través de unas cortinas de organza cuando aparece un moderno templo del consumo en tonos verdes. Unos paneles de hormigón pintados de amarillo que súbitamente conforman una franja que se asocia con la identidad de un bar de copas y comidas. Unos troncos de abedul con su blanco y negro característico hacen las veces de biombo al tiempo que le da al entorno un toque natural. Una alfombra en color rojo fuego se revela como un mullido revestimiento para suelos a base de granulado de goma y convierte un vestíbulo gris en una sala de estar de carácter urbano.

Contemporary Color Design presenta en sentido literal una colorida mezcla de arquitectos de todo el mundo y de sus proyectos. Manifestaciones con total convicción, reflexiones sugerentes, experimentos ingenuos, conceptos llenos de vida y aproximaciones tímidas que, de forma eficaz y focalizada, buscan descollar mediante el uso del color.

La couleur en architecture est le thème du moment. Après une longue phase au cours de laquelle simplicité et rationalité donnaient le ton pour le design, et les couleurs des matériaux se contentaient, dans le meilleur des cas, de compléter le blanc, le noir et le gris, de nombreux architectes se tournent de plus en plus vers le monde des couleurs.

Il semble n'y avoir aucune limite à la richesse des idées, à la créativité et au choix des couleurs. Les projets présentés ici illustrent des perceptions et des démarches très différentes : de l'interprétation des couleurs de l'entreprise comme expression architecturale de son identité, aux concepts développés de manière sensible, en considérant les effets de la couleur sur les utilisateurs et le milieu. Les effets de la couleur et la réaction qu'elle provoque sont subjectifs : pour cette raison seulement, les architectes choisissent des couleurs variées pour leurs bâtiments et ce choix ne suit pas toujours des lois strictes. Cependant, il existe des correspondances générales dans les perceptions, sur lesquelles les concepteurs s'accordent.

Le jaune - couleur du soleil et de la lumière - est apprécié pour sa brillance. Il donne un aspect clair et accueillant aux pièces. Le jaune diffuse le zeste de la vie et, plus important, encourage la communication. Cela en fait l'ambiance appropriée pour un bar à cocktail comme le Nama à Stuttgart.
Le rouge est la couleur de la chaleur et surtout, de l'amour. Mais le sang aussi est rouge. Le feu et les batailles sont également liés à cette couleur, qui prévient contre les dangers en les signalant. Le théâtre rouge du Lelystadt, au cœur de la construction, dégage cette chaleur. Son modèle est le soleil couchant sur la ville néerlandaise d'Ijsselmeer. Par ailleurs, Dock 47 - le principal immeuble de bureaux entre le quartier des boîtes de nuit et le port d'Hambourg - domine fièrement les rues en rouge signal.
Le bleu évoque l'immensité - celle de l'océan et du ciel. C'est une couleur claire qui symbolise l'intellect et l'esprit. Ainsi, le bleu des carreaux de l'école d'Heilbronn représente bien plus que la couleur préférée de l'architecte. Il symbolise l'apprentissage. Au White Blue Black à Tokyo - un bâtiment résidentiel pour bibliophiles - le savoir collectionné repose uniquement sur des étagères bleues.
Le vert, c'est la nature, la base de nos vies, une couleur très reposante. Le vert est entre la froideur du bleu et la chaleur du jaune : il harmonise et équilibre. Il semble naturel que des institutions éducatives soient peintes de cette couleur équilibrante : l'acquisition de connaissance et d'expérience de vie est vue comme un processus naturel de croissance. Cependant, les architectes du parking souterrain sur la berge du Rhin à Mainz amènent la prairie dans un monde souterrain de béton gris. Pour les conducteurs qui arrivent, le vert anticipe ce qui les attend sur la berge du Rhin.

Les concepts des architectes présentés ici vont bien plus loin que le simple fait de peindre des murs d'une certaine couleur. Les matériaux et les couleurs se complètent et communiquent mutuellement. Ils offrent aux observateurs une nouvelle perspective de l'intérieur et de l'extérieur : le jardin d'un monastère ancien luit à travers des draperies d'organza et plonge un temple moderne du consumérisme dans une lumière verte. Des panneaux de coffrage de béton brut reçoivent une couche de peinture jaune et apparaissent soudain comme une bande porteuse d'identité entre le bar à cocktail et le snack bar. Des troncs de bouleaux, avec leur noir et blanc caractéristique, servent de cloison semi-transparente et confèrent à ce qui les entoure une touche naturelle. Un tapis rouge-feu s'avère être un revêtement de sol mou en granulés de caoutchouc, qui transforme une place grise en salle de séjour municipale.

Contemporary Color Design présente un mélange - littéralement - coloré d'architectes du monde entier et leurs projets : des déclarations assumées, une nourriture stimulante pour l'esprit, des expériences sans inhibition, des concepts pleins d'humour et de vie, ainsi que des démarches plus discrètes mais efficaces qui mettent l'accent sur une couleur particulière.

Il colore nell'architettura è un tema d'attualità. Dopo una lunga fase, durante la quale erano la linearità e la razionalità a segnare il design e tutt'al più erano i colori dei materiali a integrare l'immagine del bianco, del nero e del grigio, da un po' di tempo molti architetti si sono rivolti in modo marcato al mondo dei colori.

Non ci sembrano essere limiti alla ricchezza di idee, alla creatività e alla scelta dei colori. I progetti presentati testimoniano delle interpretazioni e dei modi di procedere molto differenti tra loro: dalla trasposizione dei colori dell'azienda come espressione della Corporate Identity nell'architettura fino a concetti elaborati in modo sensibile, che si occupano della questione dell'effetto che ha il colore sull'utente e l'ambiente circostante. L'effetto e la sensazione del colore sono soggettivi: già per questa ragione la scelta di colori fatta dagli architetti per i loro edifici è varia e non segue sempre delle regole rigorose. Eppure esistono ancora delle concordanze generalmente valide nelle percezioni che riprendono anche i progettisti.

Il giallo, in quanto colore del sole e della luce, viene apprezzato grazie alla sua luminosità. Gli spazi appaiono chiari e gentili. Il giallo irradia la gioia di vivere - e favorisce soprattutto la comunicazione. Quindi il giusto ambiente per un cocktail-bar e una foodbar come la Nama a Stoccarda.
Il rosso è il colore del calore e soprattutto dell'amore. Ma anche il sangue è rosso. Il fuoco e la battaglia sono legati a questo colore, che avverte del pericolo come rosso segnaletico. La sala rossa del teatro a Lelystadt, in quanto cuore dell'edificio, emana questo calore. Il modello seguito è il sole al tramonto sopra la città olandese sul mare Ijssel. Il Dock 47, l'edificio dominante composto da uffici tra il quartiere di divertimento e il porto di Amburgo, si impone invece con un rosso segnaletico nello spazio stradale.
Il blu rievoca un'associazione di vastità - come il mare e il cielo. E' un colore chiaro, che rappresenta la mente e lo spirito. Il blu della scuola piastrellata a Heilbronn rappresenta così ben più del colore preferito dall'architetto. E' il simbolo dell'istruzione. Nel White Blue Black a Tokyo, un'abitazione per amanti dei libri, tutta la conoscenza raccolta si poggia solamente su scaffali blu.
Il verde è la natura, il fondamento della nostra vita, che in quanto colore agisce come rilassante. Il verde si trova tra il blu freddo e il giallo caldo; armonizza ed equilibra. Sembra essere un fatto naturale, che gli allestimenti formativi vengano tenuti in questo colore equilibrante: l'aumento della conoscenza e dell'esperienza di vita come processo di crescita naturale. Gli architetti del garage sotterraneo sulle sponde del Reno a Magonza portano il prato in un mondo sotterraneo di grigio cemento. Il verde anticipa al guidatore in arrivo la gioia di quello che lo aspetta sulla sponda del Reno.

I concetti degli architetti presentati vanno ben oltre la semplice pittura colorata delle pareti. I materiali e il colore si integrano e comunicano tra loro. Aprono agli osservatori una nuova visione sull'esterno e sull'interno: un giardino di un convento storico risplende attraverso delle tende di organza e immerge un tempio del consumo moderno in luce verde. Delle grezze cassette di cemento vengono dipinte di giallo e assumono improvvisamente l'aspetto di un nastro che creano l'identità tra il cocktail-bar e lo snackbar. Dei tronchi di betulla nel loro caratteristico bianco-nero servono da divisori semitrasparenti dello spazio e donano all'ambiente una nota naturale. Un tappeto rosso fuoco si rivela essere un rivestimento del pavimento di granulato e trasforma un grigio atrio in un salone cittadino.

Il Contemporary Color Design presenta - in senso letterario - una miscela variopinta di architetti internazionali e i loro progetti. Dichiarazioni consapevoli, spunti di riflessione stimolanti, sperimenti spontanei, interpretazioni spiritose e piene di gioia di vivere, oltre ad accostamenti discreti, che pongono degli accenti mirati di colore pieni di effetto.

03 MÜNCHEN GBR | MUNICH, GERMANY

Website	www.03muenchen.de
Project	Yellow Exhibition pavillion
Location	Munich, Germany
Year of Completion	2005
Building Materials	Aluminum frame covered with plastic sheet
Color Specification	Luminous yellow
Photo Credits	Simone Rosenberg

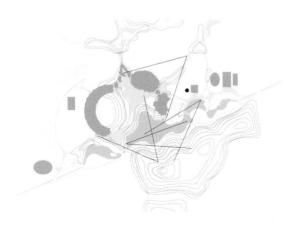

Not dark like a camera obscura but glowing in yellow to a large extent—yet the principle is similar: It's possible to walk through some of the exhibit objects for the supporting program of the BUGA 2005. A window, which the architects 03 München have precisely arranged, shows visitors a defined sector of the landscape that becomes imprinted in the memory. Elements of the classic landscape park such as buildings, statues, and columns mark the focal points, intersections, and lines of sight. This inspired the architects in their objects, which emphasize a special place in the park. The walls serve as exhibition areas and inform visitors about the history of the origins and concepts behind the park.

Nicht dunkel wie eine Camera Obscura, sondern weithin gelb leuchtend – aber ein doch ähnliches Prinzip: Einige der Ausstellungsobjekte zum Rahmenprogramm der BUGA 2005 sind begehbar. Ein Fenster, das die Architekten 03 München präzise anordnen, zeigt den Besuchern einen festgelegten Ausschnitt der Landschaft, der sich im Gedächtnis einprägt. Elemente aus klassischen Landschaftsparks wie Gebäude, Statuen und Säulen markieren Blickpunkte, Kreuzungen und Sichtachsen. Dies inspirierte die Architekten zu ihren Objekten, die einen besonderen Ort im Park hervorheben. Die Wände dienen als Ausstellungsfläche und informieren über die Entstehungsgeschichte und die Konzepte, die hinter den Parks stehen.

No es sombrío como una cámara oscura, sino que se ilumina en tonos amarillos. Aunque el principio es el mismo: algunos de los objetos exhibidos dentro del programa del BUGA 2005 son transitables. Una ventana, dispuesta de forma precisa por los arquitectos de 03 München, muestra al visitante una porción determinada del paisaje que se queda grabada en la memoria. Elementos típicos de un parque, como son los edificios, las estatuas o las columnas, fijan el punto de mira, las intersecciones y los ejes panorámicos. De este modo, los arquitectos encontraron la inspiración para enfocar los objetos y resaltar así un lugar concreto del parque. Las paredes hacen de superficies expositivas y muestran información sobre los orígenes y los conceptos que sirven de base a los parques.

Non pas sombre comme une camera obscura mais plutôt jaune brillant – cependant le principe est similaire : il est possible de traverser certains des objets exposés pour le programme du BUGA 2005. Une fenêtre, que les architectures de 03 München ont aménagée avec précision, montre aux visiteurs un secteur défini du paysage qui s'imprime dans la mémoire. Les éléments du parc paysager classique comme les bâtiments, les statues et les colonnes indiquent les points de focalisation, les intersections et les angles de vision. Cela a inspiré les architectes pour leurs objets, qui soulignent un lieu particulier du parc. Les murs servent de zones d'exposition et informent les visiteurs de l'histoire et des concepts à l'origine du parc.

Non così scura come una camera oscura, ma in un giallo luminoso che si vede da lontano – eppure si tratta di un principio simile: alcuni degli oggetti esposti durante la BUGA 2005 sono accessibili. Una finestra che gli architetti 03 München mettono in un ordine preciso, mostra ai visitatori uno scorcio definito del paesaggio, che resta impresso nella mente. Gli elementi di parchi paesaggistici classici come edifici, statue e colonne segnano i punti prospettici, gli incroci e le assi visive. Questo è quello che ha ispirato gli architetti a produrre i loro oggetti, che esaltano un punto particolare del parco. Le pareti servono da superficie espositiva e informano sulla storia delle origini e sui concetti che si trovano dietro ai parchi.

AAVP ARCHITECTURE | PARIS, FRANCE
BASE PAYSAGISTES | PARIS, FRANCE

Website	www.aavp-architectes.com
Project	Indaten 355 A
	(Culture and recreation facilities—rehabilitation and extension of the park's recreation and culture facilities)
Chief of Project	Roel Dehoorne Architecte
Location	Parc des Près de Lyon, Ville de La Chapelle-Saint-Luc, France
Year of Completion	2007
Building Materials	Expanded metal galvanized steel
Color Specifications	Black and colorful tile floor
Photo Credits	Olivier Helbert & aavparchitecture, Paris

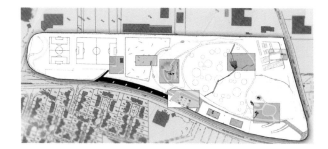

In the park of La-Chapelle-Saint Luc in the Champagne, six objects glow even without electricity. The structures of the urban park are unmistakable with their natural radiance. The sports fields and places of cultural interest—such as the Boulodrome or the dressing rooms of the soccer players, achieve a strong harmony with the newly designed park landscape through their color scheme. Since colors are "alive" in nature, which means that they change, the aavp architecture architects have relied on rough, weatherproof materials, especially the structural steel Indaten 355A. Its surface oxidizes to red rust in conjunction with oxygen. The planners set accents with natural shades from the surrounding environment—fuchsia, rose red, and tobacco.

Im Park von La-Chapelle-Saint Luc in der Champagne leuchten sechs Objekte, auch ohne Elektrizität. Mit natürlicher Strahlkraft machen die Bauten die städtische Grünanlage unverwechselbar. Die Sport- und Kulturstätten, wie das Boulodrome oder die Umkleiden der Fußballer, erreichen durch ihre Farbgebung eine starke Übereinstimmung mit der neugestalteten Parklandschaft. Da Farben in der Natur „leben", das heißt sich verändern, setzten die Architekten aavp architecture auf rohe, wetterbeständige Materialien, vor allem auf den Baustahl Indaten 355A, dessen Oberfläche in Verbindung mit Sauerstoff zu Rotrost oxidiert. Akzente setzen die Planer mit Naturtönen aus der Umgebung – Fuchsia, Rosenrot, Tabak.

En el parque de La-Chapelle-Saint Luc en la Champagne brillan seis objetos, incluso sin electricidad. La radiación natural de estas estructuras las hace inconfundibles dentro de este parque urbano. Los lugares de interés cultural o los recintos deportivos tales como el Boulodrome o los vestuarios de los futbolistas están en perfecta armonía con el nuevo diseño del parque gracias a la combinación cromática. Puesto que los colores "viven" en la naturaleza, lo que significa que cambian, los arquitectos de aavp architecture se han decidido por materiales toscos y resistentes a la intemperie, especialmente en el caso del Indaten 355A, cuya superficie adquiere un tono rojizo por oxidación. Los planificadores han enfatizado sus diseños con tonos naturales del entorno como fucsia, rojo rosado y tabaco.

Dans le Parc de La-Chapelle-Saint Luc, en Champagne, six objets luisent sans électricité. Les structures du parc urbain sont inmanquables grâce à leur rayonnement naturel. Grâce à leur thème de couleurs, les terrains de sport et les lieux d'intérêt cuturel, comme le Boulodrome ou les vestiaires des joueurs de foot, sont en grande harmonie avec le parc paysager nouvellement dessiné. Comme les couleurs sont « vivantes » dans la nature, ce qui signifie qu'elles changent, les architectes d'aavp architecture se sont basés sur des matériaux bruts, imperméables, et particulièrement l'acier structurel Indaten 355A. Sa surface s'oxyde et se couvre de rouille rouge au contact de l'oxygène. Les concepteurs donnent le ton avec les teintes naturelles qu'on retrouve dans l'environnement - fuschia, rouge rosé et tabac.

Nel parco di La-Chapelle-Saint Luc nella Champagne risplendono sei oggetti, anche senza elettricità. Con una forza di irradiazione naturale le costruzioni rendono inconfondibile l'area verde cittadina. Il centro sportivo e quello culturale, come il Boulodrome o gli spogliatoi dei calciatori raggiungono con la loro colorazione una forte concordanza con il paesaggio del parco ristrutturato. Dato che i colori "vivono" nella natura, il che vuol dire che si modificano, gli architetti di aavp architecture hanno puntato su materiali grezzi e resistenti alle intemperie, in particolare sull'acciaio da costruzione Indaten 355A, la cui superficie si ossida in ruggine rossa a contatto con l'ossigeno. I progettisti hanno posto degli accenti con toni naturali dei dintorni - fucsia, rosa e tabacco.

AAVP ARCHITECTURE | PARIS, FRANCE

Website	www.aavp-architectes.com
Project	MQP, Maison de Quartier & Bibliothèque
Location	Parc du Jardin Parisien, Clamart, France
Year of Completion	2007
Building Materials	Wood-veneer panels, footbridge plates of polycarbonate matt and clear, stained cement plaster, stained concrete floor, wall coating with wax-paper wallpaper and colored paint
Color Specifications	Beige, light and dark gray in contrast to red wall and floor surfaces.
Photo Credits	Olivier Helbert & aavp architecture, Paris

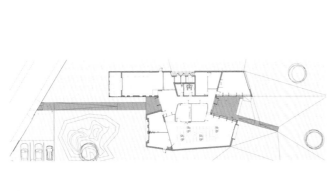

The district center MQP in Clamart is a meeting place and offers space to the community and a small library. The building connects the city in a southerly direction with the park in the north. A long, straight path leads onto the narrow property toward the building. The projecting roof with its corrugated metal that marks the main entrance reflects the circulation of coming and going that takes place in the building. In the design of the walls, ceiling, and floor, aavp architecture set subdued tones such as beige, light gray, and dark gray in a contrast with exquisite colors, such as walls with wax-paper wallpaper and red wall and floor surfaces. The inner court opens up to the green—the park.

Das Stadtteilzentrum MQP in Clamart ist Treffpunkt und bietet Raum für die Gemeinschaft und eine kleine Bibliothek. Das Gebäude verbindet die Stadt in südlicher Richtung mit dem Park im Norden. Ein langer, geradliniger Weg führt auf dem schmalen Grundstück zu dem Gebäude hin. Das Vordach, das den Haupteingang markiert, spiegelt mit seinem gewellten Metall die Zirkulation des Kommens und Gehens wider, das in dem Haus stattfindet. In der Wand-, Decken- und Bodengestaltung setzen aavp architecture zurückhaltende Töne wie Beige, Hell- und Dunkelgrau in Kontrast zu edlen Farben, so etwa Wände mit Wachspapiertapeten und roten Wand- und Bodenflächen. Der Innenhof öffnet sich zum Grün – dem Park.

El centro del barrio de MQP en Clamart es un punto de encuentro. Dispone de salas para la comunidad y de una biblioteca. El edificio une la ciudad en dirección sur con el parque en dirección norte. Un camino largo y rectilíneo se dirige desde el angosto terreno hacia el edificio. El alpende, que marca la entrada principal, refleja mediante su metal ondulado el ir y venir que tiene lugar en el inmueble. Los miembros de aavp architecture han utilizado en paredes, techos y suelos tonos templados como el beige o el gris claro y oscuro, en contraposición a los colores más señoriales, como las paredes con papel encerado o los suelos y las paredes en rojo. El patio interior se abre al verde del parque.

La maison de quartier MQP de Clamart est un lieu de rencontre, offrant un espace à la communauté, avec une petite bibliothèque. Le bâtiment connecte la ville dans la direction sud avec le parc au nord. Un long sentier droit mène à l'étroite propriété vers le bâtiment. L'avant-toit de métal ondulé qui indique l'entrée principale reflète le va et vient dans le bâtiment. Pour le design des murs, du plafond et du sol, aavp architecture a choisi des tons discrets comme le beige, le gris clair et le gris foncé dans un contraste avec des couleurs délicates, notamment des murs couverts de papier-peint ciré et des sols et des murs rouges. La cour intérieure s'ouvre vers le vert – le parc.

Il centro del quartiere MQP a Clamart è un punto di ritrovo e offre spazio per la comunità e una piccola biblioteca. L'edificio collega la città verso sud con il parco a nord. Una strada lunga e diritta conduce attraverso un terreno stretto verso l'edificio. La tettoia che segna l'entrata principale, rispecchia, con il suo metallo ondulato, la circolazione dell'andare e venire che ha luogo nella casa. Nella strutturazione delle pareti, dei soffitti e dei pavimenti i aavp architecture hanno puntato su toni discreti come beige, grigio chiaro e grigio scuro in contrasto con colori nobili, come per esempio le pareti con tappezzeria in carta cerata e superfici rosse per le pareti e i pavimenti. Il cortile interno si apre al verde – al parco.

AAVP ARCHITECTURE | PARIS, FRANCE
ANTONIO VIRGA ARCHITECTE | PARIS, FRANCE

Website	www.aavp-architectes.com
Project	RAG, Casa do Portugal
Chief of Project	Nicolas Jouard Architecte
Location	Paris, France
Year of Completion	2007
Building Materials	Extra light glass, golden lacquered aluminum, stained concrete, birch plywood sheeting, embossed paper and painted panels (red, black, plum, gray), black Eternit Glasal panelling, silvery curtains
Color Specifications	Interior: red, orange, green; Exterior: gold
Photo Credits	Olivier Helbert & aavp architecture, Paris

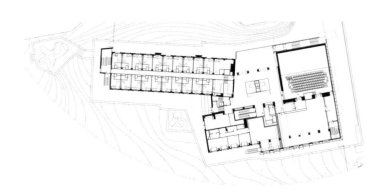

The international student quarters in Paris have gained another national house: Portugal presents itself with the project RAG. The structure with 170 rooms, a theater, and a showroom is located near the Brazilian house by Lucio Costa and Oscar Niemeyer, as well as the Swiss house by Le Corbusier. Both halves of the RAG building are designed in a dark gray. A wide façade skin, imitating the mosaics typical of Portugal, provides shade. In the interior, aavp architecture has picked up a melancholy Portuguese flair: dark floors, walls in the colors of red, eggplant, brown, and black. Baroque-like embossed wallpaper continues the color scheme.

Die internationale Studentensiedlung in Paris ist um ein Nationen-Haus reicher: Portugal präsentiert sich mit dem Projekt RAG. Das Bauwerk mit 170 Zimmern, Theater und Ausstellungsraum befindet sich in der Nachbarschaft des brasilianischen Hauses, von Lucio Costa und Oscar Niemeyer, sowie des Schweizer Hauses von Le Corbusier. Beide RAG-Gebäudehälften sind in einem dunklen Grau angelegt. Eine zweite Fassadenhaut, dem für Portugal typischen Mosaik nachempfunden, spendet Schatten. Im Inneren greifen aavp architecture einen melancholischen portugiesischen Flair auf: dunkle Fußböden, die Wände in den Farben Rot, Aubergine, Braun und Schwarz. Barock anmutende Prägetapeten führen die Farbgebung weiter.

La comunidad internacional de residencias estudiantiles de París tiene un nuevo miembro: Portugal, que se presentó con su Proyecto RAG. El edificio consta de 170 habitaciones, teatro y sala de exposiciones y se sitúa al costado de la casa brasileña obra de Lucio Costa y Oscar Niemeyer, y de la casa suiza de Le Corbusier. Las dos mitades del edificio RAG son de color gris oscuro. Una segunda capa de la fachada, a imitación de los típicos mosaicos portugueses, genera sombra. Los de aavp architecture han apostado en el interior por la melancolía portuguesa: pavimento oscuro y paredes en rojo, berenjena, marrón y negro. El papel pintado con motivos barrocos continúa la misma línea cromática.

Les résidences pour étudiants étrangers de Paris ont gagné une nouvelle maison nationale : le Portugal présente le projet RAG. La structure comportant 170 chambres, un théâtre et une salle d'exposition, est située près de la maison brésilienne de Lucio Costa et Oscar Niemeyer, et de la maison suisse de Le Corbusier. Les deux moitiés du bâtiment RAG sont dessinées en un gris foncé. Un revêtement de façade blanc, imitant les mosaïques typiques du Portugal, procure de l'ombre. A l'intérieur, aavp architecture a rendu le génie mélancolique portugais : sols noirs, murs rouges, aubergine, marron et noirs. Un papier peint gaufré de style baroque prolonge l'agencement des couleurs.

La residenza studentesca internazionale a Parigi si è arricchita di una casa-nazione: il Portogallo si presenta con il progetto RAG. La costruzione con 170 camere, un teatro e un locale per le mostre si trova nelle vicinanze della casa brasiliana, di Lucio Costa e Oscar Niemeyer, oltre alla casa svizzera di Le Corbusier. Tutte e due le metà dell'edificio RAG sono costruite in un grigio scuro. Un secondo strato di facciata, che ricrea il tipico mosaico portoghese, offre dell'ombra. All'interno aavp architecture ha richiamato una nota melanconica portoghese: pavimenti scuri, pareti in rosso, violetto, marrone e nero. Una tappezzeria in rilievo che ricorda il barocco continua la colorazione.

ARCHITEKTEN PROF. ARNO LEDERER,
JÓRUNN RAGNARSDÓTTIR, MARC OEI | STUTTGART, GERMANY

Website	www.lederer-ragnarsdottir-oei.de
Project	Gustav von Schmoller School
Location	Heilbronn, Germany
Year of Completion	2003
Building Materials	Reinforced concrete construction, prefabricated concrete arches
Color Specifications	Dark blue ceramic tile façade; seating niches painted in yellow, red and green
Photo Credits	Roland Halbe, Stuttgart

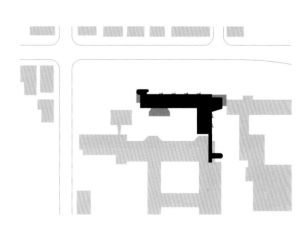

The viewer only trusts the second glance—a building completely covered in tile and in blue on top of it! Ceramics have a history in Heilbronn. During the 1950s and 1960s, many houses were built here with this façade decoration that was typical of this period. The architects Lederer + Ragnarsdóttir + Oei continued this with absolute determination at the vocational school and worked with the manufacturers to develop a ceramic tile that satisfies their demands: the slightly curved surface of the tiles provides elegant color and light play for the façade covering more than 9,843 sq. ft. With the color, the Stuttgart architects refer to Alvar Aalto, who decisively influenced the design and architecture of the 1960s.

Der Betrachter traut erst dem zweiten Blick – ein Gebäude komplett gefliest und zwar in Blau! Die Keramik hat Geschichte in Heilbronn. In den 50er- und 60er-Jahren entstanden dort viele Häuser mit dem für diese Zeit typischen Fassadenschmuck. Die Architekten Lederer + Ragnarsdóttir + Oei führten dies in aller Konsequenz an der Berufsschule weiter und entwickelten mit den Herstellern eine Keramikfliese, die ihren Ansprüchen gerecht wird: die leicht gewölbte Oberfläche der Fliesen verleiht der mehr als 3000 m^2 umfassenden Fassade ein elegantes Farb- und Lichtspiel. Mit der Farbe beziehen sich die Stuttgarter Architekten auf Alvar Aalto, der Design und Architektur der 60er-Jahre maßgeblich beeinflusste.

Habrá que echarle un segundo vistazo a este edificio completamente alicatado… ¡de color azul! La cerámica forma parte de la historia de la ciudad alemana de Heilbronn. En los años 50 y 60 se construyeron muchas viviendas con fachadas decoradas de esta forma, por entonces típica. Los arquitectos Lederer + Ragnarsdóttir + Oei lo llevaron hasta las últimas consecuencias en este instituto de formación profesional. Junto al fabricante, desarrollaron unos azulejos que cumplieran con sus expectativas. La superficie ligeramente abovedada del alicatado cubre una fachada de más de 3.000 m^2 dotándola de un elegante juego de luz y color. Estos arquitectos de Stuttgart hacen referencia con el uso del color a Alvar Aalto, de gran influencia en el diseño y la arquitectura de los años 60.

L'observateur n'y croit qu'au second coup d'œil – un bâtiment entièrement couvert de carreaux, et bleu par-dessus le reste ! Les céramiques ont une histoire à Heilbronn. Pendant les années 50 et 60, de nombreuses maisons y étaient construites avec cette décoration de façade typique de l'époque. Les architectes Lederer + Ragnarsdóttir + Oei ont perpétué cette tradition avec une détermination absolue pour ce centre de formation professionnelle, et ont travaillé avec les fabricants pour créer un carreau de céramique qui satisfasse leurs exigences : la surface légèrement courbe des carreaux fournit une couleur élégante et un jeu de lumières pour la façade d'une surface de plus de 3 000 m^2. Avec cette couleur, les architectes de Stuttgart se réfèrent à Alvar Aalto, dont l'influence fut décisive pour le design et l'architecture des années 60.

L'osservatore deve guardare una seconda volta per crederci – un edificio completamente piastrellato e precisamente in blu! La ceramica ha storia a Heilbronn. Negli anni '50 e '60 lì sono state costruite molte case con le decorazioni della facciata tipiche di quel tempo. Gli architetti Lederer + Ragnarsdóttir + Oei hanno continuato questa tradizione in modo conseguente nella scuola professionale e hanno sviluppato insieme ai produttori una piastrella in ceramica che corrisponde alle loro esigenze: la superficie leggermente bombata delle piastrelle regala alla facciata, con i suoi abbondanti 3000 m^2, un gioco elegante di colori e luci. Con il colore gli architetti di Stoccarda fanno riferimento ad Alvar Aalto, che ha influenzato in modo determinante il design e l'architettura degli anni '60.

ARCHITEKTENGEMEINSCHAFT ZIMMERMANN | DRESDEN, GERMANY

Website	www.ag-zimmermann.de
Project	Kirchgemeindezentrum (Parish Center)
Location	Leipzig-Thonberg, Germany
Year of Completion	2007
Building Materials	Reinforced concrete construction
Color Specifications	Colored glass
Photo Credits	Thomas Richter, Halle/Saale

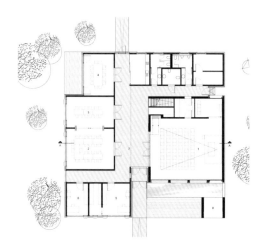

The **intention was** for the parish center was to be bright and inviting, a place of communication that simultaneously offers oases of silence. The Zimmermann architect association "folded" a continuous room structure from an imaginary surface, arranging the church hall at its center. The planners gave the simple room a special atmosphere by providing it with a circumferential window panel. Printed glass corresponds with the seasonal colors of nature and provides a play of light. On the exterior, the building sculpture appears in a different form on every side. The illuminated church hall shines at night through the colored stripe motif. The bell tower serves as a landmark.

Hell und einladend sollte das Gemeindezentrum sein, ein Ort der Kommunikation, der gleichzeitig Oasen der Stille bietet. Die Architektengemeinschaft Zimmermann „faltete" aus einer imaginären Fläche ein kontinuierliches Raumgefüge, in dessen Mitte sie den Kirchsaal anordneten. Dem schlichten Raum verleihen die Planer eine besondere Atmosphäre, indem sie ein umlaufendes Fensterband vorsehen. Das bedruckte Glas entspricht den jahreszeitlichen Farben der Natur und sorgt für ein Lichtspiel. Außen erscheint die Gebäudeskulptur zu allen Seiten in anderer Form, und abends tritt der illuminierte Kirchenraum durch das farbige Streifenmotiv in Erscheinung. Der Glockenturm dient als Erkennungszeichen.

El centro parroquial había de ser luminoso y acogedor, un lugar para la comunicación que al tiempo fuera un oasis de silencio. El colectivo de arquitectos Zimmermann "plegó" una estructura espacial continua a partir de una superficie imaginaria, y en el centro dispusieron la nave de la iglesia. A este espacio tan sencillo lo dotaron de una atmósfera muy especial gracias a un gran ventanal corrido que lo circundaba. El cristal estampado representa los colores de la naturaleza en sus diferentes estaciones y crea un juego de luces. Desde fuera, la forma de la construcción es diferente al cambiar de perspectiva. De noche, la nave de la iglesia se ilumina a listas. El campanario es la seña de identidad.

L'objectif du Centre Paroissial était d'être à la fois brillant et attirant, un lieu de communication proposant aussi des oasis de silence. L'association d'architectes Zimmermann a « plié » une structure de pièce continue depuis une surface imaginaire, plaçant la salle paroissiale en son centre. Les concepteurs ont donné à cette pièce simple une atmosphère particulière en la dotant d'un panneau fenêtre périphérique. Le verre imprimé correspond avec les couleurs saisonnières de la nature et joue avec la lumière. A l'extérieur, la sculpture du bâtiment apparaît sous une forme différente de chaque côté. La salle paroissiale illuminée brille dans la nuit à travers le motif de rayures colorées. Le clocher sert de repère à la salle.

Il centro della comunità doveva essere chiaro e invitante, un luogo per la comunicazione che al contempo offriva delle oasi del silenzio. L'associazione di architetti Zimmermann ha "ripiegato" una struttura dello spazio continuativa ricavata da una superficie immaginaria, e al suo centro hanno inserito la sala della chiesa. I progettisti hanno conferito alla stanza sobria un'atmosfera particolare prevedendo un nastro di finestre che corre intorno. Il vetro stampato corrisponde ai colori delle stagioni presenti in natura e crea un gioco di luci. All'esterno la scultura dell'edificio appare per ogni lato in una forma diversa e la sera il locale illuminato della chiesa emerge attraverso il motivo a righe colorato. Il campanile serve da segno di riconoscimento.

RYUICHI ASHIZAWA ARCHITECTS & ASSOCIATES | OSAKA, JAPAN

Website	www.r-a-architects.com
Project	Vajra Forest
Location	Osaka, Japan
Year of Completion	1999
Building Materials	Wood, glass, steel, mortar, acrylic resin
Color specification	Colored glass
Photo Credits	Kaori Ichikawa, Osaka

Light and colored glass create a phenomenon in the shop at the center of Osaka: 24 mirrored glass room dividers, each in a different shade, "paint" the wall and floor with daylight as the sun changes its position throughout the day. The room on the fourth floor of an office building receives much daylight from all sides. The Ryuichi Ashizawa Architects have designed the commercial premises in a way that it is suitable for various uses such a gallery, event space, or exhibition area. They understand the room to be a structure with moveable elements that offer personnel and guests the possibility of adapting the space to their needs instead of a design set in stone.

Licht und farbiges Glas sorgen in dem Shop im Zentrum von Osaka für ein Phänomen: 24 verspiegelte Glas-Raumteiler, alle in anderen Farbtönen, „malen" mit Tageslicht auf Wand und Boden während die Sonne über den Tag hinweg ihre Position verändert. Der Raum im dritten Geschoss eines Geschäftshauses empfängt von allen Seiten aus viel Tageslicht. Die Ryuichi Ashizawa Architects gestalten die Geschäftsräume so, dass sie unterschiedlichen Nutzungen, wie zum Beispiel als Galerie, Event- oder als Ausstellungsfläche, gerecht wird. Sie verstehen den Raum nicht als festgelegtes Design, sondern als Struktur mit beweglichen Elementen, die dem Personal und den Gästen die Möglichkeit bieten, den Raum auf ihre Bedürfnisse hin anzupassen.

La luz y los cristales tintados crean todo un fenómeno en esta tienda del centro de de la ciudad japonesa de Osaka. 24 pantallas de cristal reflectante, cada una en un tono distinto, "pintan" paredes y suelos con luz natural conforme cambia el sol de posición a lo largo del día. Este espacio situado en la tercera planta de un edificio de oficinas recibe la luz desde todos los ángulos. Los arquitectos de Bosque Urbano han diseñado este local comercial capaz de albergar diferentes usos: galería, sala de actos o de exposiciones. Entienden este local no como un diseño inalterable, sino como una estructura de elementos móviles que ofrece al personal y a los invitados la posibilidad de adaptar el espacio a sus necesidades.

La lumière et le verre coloré créent un phénomène dans la boutique du centre d'Osaka : 24 cloisons en verre miroir, chacune d'une teinte différente, « peignent » le mur et le sol avec la lumière du jour au fur et à mesure que le soleil change de position. La pièce, au quatrième étage de l'immeuble de bureaux, reçoit énormément de lumière de tous les côtés. Les architectes d'Urban Forest Architects ont conçu les locaux commerciaux de manière à ce qu'ils conviennent pour différents usages : galerie, salle de spectacle ou lieu d'exposition. Ils voient la pièce comme une structure avec des éléments mobiles qui offrent au personnel et aux visiteurs la possibilité d'adapter l'espace à leurs besoins, plutôt qu'un design figé dans la pierre.

La luce e il vetro colorato creano un fenomeno nel negozio al centro di Osaka: 24 divisori in vetro a specchio, tutti con diverse tonalità di colore, "dipingono" sulle pareti e sul pavimento attraverso la luce del giorno, mentre il sole cambia la sua posizione nell'arco della giornata. Il locale al terzo piano di un palazzo per negozi riceve da tutti i lati molta luce solare. Gli architetti Urban Forest hanno progettato il locale del negozio in modo da consentire vari utilizzi come spazio per una galleria, per un evento o per una mostra. Loro non interpretano lo spazio come un progetto prestabilito, ma come struttura con elementi mobili che offrono sia al personale sia agli ospiti la possibilità di adattare lo spazio alle loro esigenze.

AT 103 | MEXICO CITY, MEXICO

Website	www.at103.net
Project	GM1607
Location	Mexico City, Mexico
Year of Completion	2005
Building Materials	Reinforced concrete construction
Color Specification	Black-pigmented concrete, synthetic-resin-bonded, pink-colored paint
Photo Credits	Adolfo Pardo, Mexico City

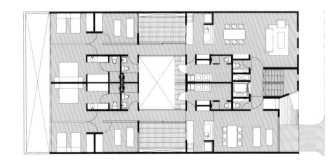

The **residential building GM 1607** accommodates eight apartments, with two set behind each other respectively lengthwise. A space between them in the middle serves the central accessibility; two "empty spaces" at the sides serve as terraces. They are covered with climbing plants, which creates a filter between the private and the public areas. The building with its raw material of black-pigmented concrete stands in close connection with the neighboring structures in Mexico City. "The soft, tender material of the entrance"—as the architects of at 103 describe the synthetic-resin-bonded, pink-colored paint—symbolizes a "fruit that has been broken open." The building is hard on the outside and soft on the inside.

Das Wohngebäude GM 1607 nimmt acht Wohnungen auf, zwei sind jeweils in Längsrichtung hintereinander geschaltet. Ein Zwischenraum in der Mitte dient zur zentralen Erschließung, zwei seitliche „Leerräume" dienen als Terrassen. Kletterpflanzen beranken sie und schaffen somit einen Filter zwischen privaten und öffentlichen Bereichen. Der Baukörper mit seinem rauen Material aus schwarz pigmentiertem Beton steht in engem Zusammenhang mit der Nachbarbebauung in Mexiko City. „Das weiche, zarte Material des Einganges" – wie die Architekten von at 103 den kunstharzgebundenen pinkfarbenen Anstrich beschreiben – versinnbildlicht eine „aufgebrochene Frucht". Das Gebäude ist außen hart und innen weich.

La construcción residencial GM 1607 da cabida a ocho viviendas. Dos se sitúan a lo largo una detrás de la otra. El espacio que queda entre ambas sirve de acceso central. Dos "espacios vacíos" laterales se utilizan de terrazas. Están cubiertas con enredaderas, creándose así un filtro que separa el área privada de la pública. La construcción, de hormigón en bruto pigmentado en negro, está íntimamente ligada a las estructuras colindantes de la Ciudad de México. "El material suave y delicado de la entrada" – tal y como describen los arquitectos de at 103 la pintura rosada de resina sintética – simboliza una "fruta que acaba de abrirse". El edificio es recio por fuera y suave por dentro.

Le bâtiment résidentiel GM 1607 abrite huit appartements, deux unités l'une derrière l'autre dans le sens de la longueur. Un espace entre eux sert d'accès central ; deux « espaces vides » sur les côtés font office de terrasse. Ils sont couverts de plantes grimpantes, qui créent un filtre entre les zones privées et publiques. Avec sa matière première, le béton coloré de pigments noirs, le bâtiment est en proche connexion avec les structures voisines à Mexico. « Le matériau mou, tendre de l'entrée » – comme les architectes de 103 décrivent la peinture rose collée à la résine synthétique – symbolise un « fruit qui s'est ouvert ». Le bâtiment est dur à l'extérieur et mou à l'intérieur.

L'edificio d'abitazione GM 1607 comprende otto appartamenti, due dei quali sono inseriti di volta in volta in direzione longitudinale uno dietro l'altro. Uno spazio nel mezzo serve per una chiusura centrale, due "vuoti" laterali servono da terrazze. Piante rampicanti le avvinghiano e creano così un filtro tra le aree private e pubbliche. Il corpo dell'edificio con il suo materiale ruvido fatto di cemento pigmentato di nero sta in stretto rapporto con la costruzione adiacente a Mexico City. "Il materiale morbido e delicato dell'ingresso" – così gli architetti di at 103 descrivono la pittura rosa legata in vetroresina – simbolizza un "frutto spaccato". L'edificio è duro all'esterno e morbido all'interno.

BEHF ARCHITEKTEN,
EBNER HASENAUER FERENCZY ZT GMBH | VIENNA, AUSTRIA

Website	www.behf.at
Project	2006Feb01
Location	Vienna, Austria
Year of Completion	2006
Building Materials	Glass, powder-coated metal, high-grade steel, carpet, organza curtains, velvet, fabric and leather wall coverings, lighting: special production in Rome, VEST, Bar, and cubes: MDF
Color Specification	Exterior: black, Interior: violet, ivory, colorfully papered dressing rooms
Photo Credits	Bruno Klomfar

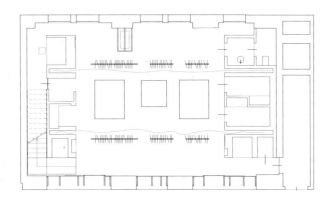

The store location by BEHF Architekten envelop customers in a friendly, cozy atmosphere that inspires them to longer, relaxed shopping sprees. The design is classic-timeless, yet also reflects the individual genius loci of Vienna's inner city as a lively shopping metropolis. The two-story store with a view of the Stephansdom cathedral is also oriented toward a historic monastery garden that shimmers green through the moveable organza curtains as they convey translucence and lightness. Arranged like furniture, the presentation cubes covered with purple fabric invite visitors to sit down. Niches, compartments, and dressing rooms are lined with splendid wallpaper materials, as rich in variations as stage settings.

Das Geschäftslokal von BEHF Architekten hüllt Kunden in eine freundliche, wohnliche Atmosphäre, die zu längeren, entspannten Einkäufen anregt. Die Gestaltung ist klassisch zeitlos, berücksichtigt aber den individuellen Genius loci von Wiens Innerer Stadt als lebendiger Einkaufsmetropole. Das zweistöckige Geschäft mit Sichtbezug zum Stephansdom orientiert sich zu einem historischen Klostergarten, der grün durch bewegliche Organza-Vorhänge schimmert, die Transluzenz und Leichtigkeit vermitteln. Wie Mobiliar arrangierte, mit lilafarbenem Stoff überzogene Präsentationskuben laden zum Sitzen ein. Nischen, Fächer und Kabinen sind mit prächtigen Tapetenstoffen ausgeschlagen, variantenreich wie Bühnenbilder.

El local comercial de BEHF Architekten envuelve al cliente en una atmósfera afable y acogedora, que induce a realizar las compras de forma pausada y relajada. La concepción es de un clasicismo atemporal que no pasa por alto el "genius loci" de Viena como una animada metrópoli de consumo. El comercio consta de dos plantas con vistas a la Catedral de San Esteban y está orientado al histórico jardín de un convento, que se deja entrever a través de unas cortinas de organza que transmiten la sensación de transparencia y ligereza. Dispuestos como si fuera mobiliario, unos cubos tapizados en lila invitan a tomar asiento. Hornacinas, compartimientos y vestidores están recubiertos con vistosos papeles pintados, tan variados como decorados.

La boutique conçue par BEHF Architekten enveloppe les clients dans une atmosphère confortable et amicale, pour des virées shopping plus longues et plus détendues. Le design est classique et indémodable, mais reflète aussi le genius loci particulier du centre ville de Vienne en tant que métropole bouillonnante du shopping. Le bâtiment sur deux niveaux, avec vue sur la cathédrale Stephansdom, donne également sur le jardin d'un monastère ancien, qui miroite en vert à travers les draperies d'organza mobiles apportant transparence et luminosité. Aménagés comme des meubles, les cubes de présentation couverts de tissu violet invitent les visiteurs à s'asseoir. Niches, compartiments et cabines d'essayage sont alignés avec de magnifiques papiers-peints, aussi riches et variés que des décors de théâtre.

Il negozio degli architetti della BEHF avvolge i clienti in una atmosfera gentile e accogliente, che stimola ad acquisti più lunghi e rilassanti. La costruzione è classica e senza tempo, ma rispetta il Genius loci individuale della città interna di Vienna nella sua qualità di metropoli vitale per gli acquisti. Il negozio su due piani con vista sul duomo di Santo Stefano si orienta verso un giardino storico di un convento, che brilla di verde attraverso delle tende movibili di organza, che trasmettono traslucidità e leggerezza. Dei cubi di presentazione, rivestiti di stoffa viola e allestiti come un mobilio, invitano a sedersi. Le nicchie, le superfici e le cabine sono rivestite di splendide stoffe di tappezzeria che sono ricche di varianti come scenografie.

BEHF ARCHITEKTEN,
EBNER HASENAUER FERENCZY ZT GMBH | VIENNA, AUSTRIA

Website	www.behf.at
Project	Fachmarktzentrum M-City
Location	Mistelbach, NÖ, Austria
Year of Completion	2003
Building Materials	Lacquered sheet metal
Color Specification	Color gradients in green (5 shades) from light green to violet, theme of camouflage in nature.
Photo Credits	Alexander Koller

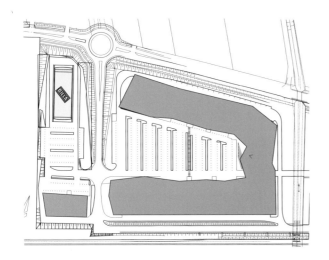

The green shopping mall on the "Grünen Wiese" (Green Meadow): In the Lower Austrian town of Mistelbach, BEHF Architekten has realized the specialty store center M-City in an emphatically functional manner. A spaciously connective projecting roof offers the necessary cold-weather protection for a piazza that—used for performances depending on the season—highlights the communication intentions of the center in addition to the mercantile purposes. The planners understand the façade color of green as a quote from nature. It gives the trade center a camouflage in the landscape. The color gradient illustrates the development of the building: a flowing form of changeability and dynamics—the green effects change through the different lighting conditions during the day and at night.

Die grüne Shoppingmall auf der „Grünen Wiese": im niederösterreichischen Mistelbach realisieren BEHF Architekten das Fachmarktzentrum M-City betont funktional. Ein großzügig verbindendes Vordach bietet den nötigen Witterungsschutz für eine Piazza, die - saisonal bespielbar - neben dem merkantilen Gedanken des Zentrums auch den der Kommunikation unterstreicht. Die Fassadenfarbe Grün verstehen die Planer als Zitat aus der Natur. Das Handelszentrum erhält durch sie eine Tarnung in der Landschaft. Der Farbverlauf verdeutlicht die Entwicklung des Gebäudes: eine fließende Form der Veränderbarkeit und Dynamik - die Grüneffekte verändern sich durch die unterschiedlichen Lichtverhältnisse bei Tag und Nacht.

Esta gran superficie de color verde en medio de un verde prado de la ciudad austriaca de Mistelbach es obra de BEHF Architekten. El centro comercial especializado M-City es muy funcional. Un alpende amplio y unido al cuerpo del edificio ofrece la suficiente protección a una plaza que, según la estación del año, remarca el carácter mercantil y comunicativo del centro. El color de la fachada, en verde, es entendido por los diseñadores como determinado por la naturaleza. El centro comercial consigue así camuflarse en el entorno. La gradación del color simboliza la evolución del edificio, con formas fluidas de carácter cambiante y dinámico. Los efectos del verde varían dependiendo de la distinta incidencia de la luz, ya sea de día o de noche.

Un centre commercial vert sur le « Grünen Wiese » (Verte Prairie) : dans la ville de Basse Autriche de Mistelbach, BEHF Architekten a réalisé le centre commercial M-City d'une manière particulièrement fonctionnelle. Un avant-toit spacieux offre la protection nécessaire contre les rigueurs du climat en formant une galerie - accueillant parfois des manifestations selon les saisons - qui met en valeur les objectifs de communication du centre, en plus de sa vocation mercantile. Les concepteurs voient la couleur verte de la façade comme une citation de la nature. Elle permet de camoufler le centre commercial dans le paysage. Les graduations de couleur illustrent le développement du bâtiment : une forme fluide de changement et de dynamique - les effets verts se transforment grâce aux différents éclairages le jour et la nuit.

Il centro commerciale verde sul "prato verde": a Mistelbach, nella Bassa Austria, gli architetti della BEHF hanno realizzato il Fachmarktzentrum M-City in modo marcatamente funzionale. Una tettoia che unisce generosamente offre la protezione necessaria contro le intemperie per una Piazza, che - sfruttabile dal punto di vista musicale in certe stagioni - sottolinea, accanto al lato commerciale, anche la comunicabilità del centro. Il colore delle facciate è stato interpretato dai progettisti come citazione della natura. Il centro commerciale ne riceve una mimetizzazione nel paesaggio. Il tracciato del colore spiega lo sviluppo dell'edificio: una forma scorrevole di modificabilità e dinamicità - gli effetti in verde variano in base alle differenti condizioni di luce del giorno e della notte.

BOTTEGA + EHRHARDT ARCHITEKTEN | STUTTGART, GERMANY

Website	www.be-arch.com
Project	Foodbar Nama
Location	Stuttgart, Germany
Year of Completion	2005
Building Materials	Birch wood, birch trunks, gray resin, filler, industrial products, black silk-screen
Photo Credits	David Franck Photographie, www.davidfranck.de

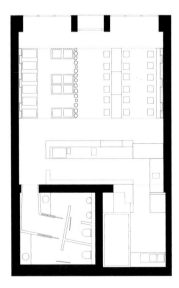

Health-food products during the day, cocktails in the evening: The Foodbar Nama in Stuttgart succeeds in the balancing act between healthy and stylish. Bottega + Ehrhardt Architekten relies on the connecting yellow color. As an identity-providing element, the room of just 164 sq. ft. has a yellow band of rough concrete formwork panels. It creates a separation from the lounge-seating area on the one side hand and from the snackbar-standing area on the other; then it runs across the ceiling with integrated lighting to form a band. Birch trunks in the characteristic black-and-white serve as a semi-transparent room divider and represent the natural elements. The counter of black concrete formwork panels and the white globe lamps match the birch motif.

Tagsüber Naturkostprodukte, abends Cocktails: die Foodbar Nama in Stuttgart schafft den Spagat zwischen gesund und stylish. Bottega + Ehrhardt Architekten setzen auf verbindendes Gelb. Der Raum von nur 50 m² erhält als identitätsstiftendes Element ein gelbes Band aus rohen Betonschaltafeln. Es grenzt zum einen den Lounge-Sitzbereich ab, bildet auf der anderen Seite den Snackbar-Stehbereich und zieht sich über die Decke, mit integrierten Leuchten, zum Band zusammen. Birkenstämme in charakteristischem Schwarzweiß dienen als semitransparenter Raumteiler und stehen für das Natürliche. Der Tresen aus schwarzen Betonschaltafeln und die weißen Kugelleuchten passen sich dem Birkenmotiv an.

De día, alimentos naturales, de noche, cócteles. El Foodbar Nama de Stuttgart (Alemania) consigue lo imposible: aunar salud y estilo. Los arquitectos Bottega + Ehrhardt se decantan por un amarillo aglutinador. El espacio de unos 50 m² cuenta como elemento identificativo con una banda amarilla de paneles de hormigón al descubierto. A un lado linda con la zona de descanso con asientos, y al otro con el área para consumir de pie, extendiéndose por el techo con iluminación integrada, conformando así toda la banda. Los troncos de abedul, con sus característicos colores blanco y negro, sirven de separación semitransparente y le dan un toque natural. Los trenzados de paneles de hormigón negros y las luminarias esféricas blancas encajan a la perfección con los detalles en abedul.

Produits diététiques pendant la journée, cocktails le soir : le Foodbar Nama de Stuttgart réussit l'équilibre entre santé et chic. Les architectes de Bottega + Ehrhardt Architekten se sont basés sur le jaune, couleur de connexion. Comme élément d'identité, la pièce de seulement 50 m² possède une bande de panneaux de coffrage de béton brut jaune. Elle crée une séparation avec la zone salon-lounge d'un côté et la zone snack bar de l'autre ; elle court ensuite à travers le plafond avec un éclairage intégré pour former une bande. Les troncs de bouleau de leur noir et blanc caractéristique servent de séparation de pièce semi-transparente et représentent les éléments naturels. Le comptoir de panneaux de coffrage en béton noir et les lampes globes blanches sont assortis au motif bouleau.

Di giorno prodotti di alimentazione naturale, la sera cocktail: la Foodbar Nama a Stoccarda riesce a spaccarsi tra il salutare e lo stilistico. Gli architetti della Bottega + Ehrhardt hanno puntato su un giallo che unisce. La stanza di soli 50 m² ha ottenuto come elemento identificativo un nastro giallo di cassette di cemento. Da un lato delimita l'area per star seduti nella lounge, dall'altro crea la zona per stare in piedi allo snackbar e si stringe con il nastro tramite il soffitto con luci integrate. I tronchi di betulla con il loro caratteristico bianconero servono da divisori semitrasparenti e rappresentano il naturale. Il bancone fatto di cassette di cemento nere e la lampada a sfera bianca si adattano al disegno delle betulle.

BOTTEGA + EHRHARDT ARCHITEKTEN | STUTTGART, GERMANY

Website	www.be-arch.com
Project	Jazzclub Bix
Location	Stuttgart, Germany
Year of Completion	2006
Building Materials	Beech heartwood, lacquered MDF, anodized aluminum (copper colors), textile curtains as room dividers
Color Specifications	Warm brown and gray color tones
Photo Credits	David Franck Photographie, www.davidfranck.de

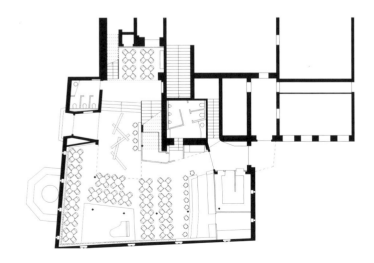

There is a jazz club in Stuttgart: The BIX is housed in a building listed on a historic register, breathing new life into it with the club's modern architecture. Two levels determine the special perception of the structure that was rebuilt in 1953. The ground floor has a spacious auditorium for live concerts while the gallery level serves as a more intimate bar and lounge area. The identity-giving element is a circumferential band of copper-colored anodized, twisted aluminum bands that frame the stage and auditorium. The intention here is to express the many-faceted variety of jazz in architectural terms. Warm brown and gray color tones, as well as the textile room dividers, also intensify the club atmosphere.

In Stuttgart steht ein Jazzclub: Das BIX ist in einem denkmalgeschützten Gebäude untergebracht und haucht ihm mit seiner modernen Architektur neues Leben ein. Zwei Ebenen bestimmen die räumliche Wahrnehmung des 1953 wieder errichteten Bauwerks. Erdgeschossig der großzügige Zuhörerraum für Live-Konzerte, die Galerieebene fungiert als intimerer Bar- und Loungebereich. Identitätsstiftendes Element ist ein umlaufendes Band aus messingfarben eloxierten, verwundenen Aluminiumbändern, das Bühne und Zuhörerraum einfasst. Der Facettenreichtum des Jazz soll hierin seinen architektonischen Ausdruck finden. Warme, braune und graue Farbtöne sowie textile Raumteiler verdichten zudem die Clubatmosphäre.

El BIX, un club de jazz en la ciudad alemana de Stuttgart, está ubicado en un edificio protegido por su valor cultural. Su moderna arquitectura le da un nuevo soplo de vida. Sus dos plantas ayudan a diferenciar los espacios de este edificio reconstruido en 1953. La planta baja es un amplio espacio para disfrutar conciertos en directo, mientras que la galería superior hace las veces de bar íntimo y área lounge. La identidad propia le viene dada por una franja compuesta por tiras viradas de aluminio anodizado en color latón que recorren todo el local, incluyendo el escenario y el espacio de conciertos. La riqueza estilística del jazz encontrará aquí su expresión arquitectónica. Tonos cálidos marrones y grises y divisores espaciales de tela contribuyen a crear ambiente en este club.

Il y a un jazz-club à Stuttgart : le BIX est abrité dans un bâtiment classé monument historique, à qui il insuffle une nouvelle vie avec son architecture moderne. Les deux niveaux déterminent la perception particulière de la structure reconstruite en 1953. Le rez-de-chaussée contient un vaste auditorium pour les concerts alors que le premier étage, plus intime, sert de bar et de lounge. L'élément donneur d'identité est un panneau périphérique de bandes d'aluminium anodisé torsadé de couleur cuivrée qui entoure la scène et l'auditorium. La volonté ici est d'exprimer la variété multi-facettes du jazz en termes architecturaux. Les tons chauds de brun et de gris, ainsi que les séparations de pièces en textile, intensifient également l'atmosphère club.

A Stoccarda c'è un Jazzclub: Il BIX è stato posizionato in un edificio posto sotto tutela dei beni artistici e lo fa rivivere con la sua architettura moderna. Due livelli definiscono la percezione spaziale della costruzione ricostruita nel 1953. Al piano terra la generosa sala d'ascolto per i concerti dal vivo, il piano adibito alla galleria funge da area intima per il bar e la lounge. L'elemento identificativo è un nastro che corre tutto intorno e che è fatto di nastri in alluminio anodizzato in color ottone e contorto, che circonda il palcoscenico e la sala d'ascolto. La ricchezza di sfaccettature del jazz può trovare qui dentro la sua espressione architettonica. Toni caldi di marrone e grigio, oltre a divisori in stoffa intensificano ulteriormente l'atmosfera da club.

BOGEVISCHS BUERO
HOFMANN RITZER ARCHITEKTEN BDA | MUNICH, GERMANY

Website	www.bogevisch.de
Project	Student Dormitory Felsennelkenanger
Project website	www.studentenwerk.mhn.de
Location	Munich, Germany
Year of Completion	2005
Building Materials	Reinforced concrete skeleton structure with ventilated front façade of fiber cement or aluminum
Color specification	Red shades – highly weatherproof powder by Tiger-Lacke.
Photo Credits	Florian Holzherr

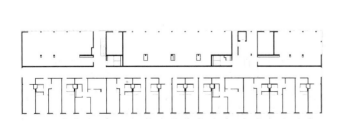

For the Munich student dormitory, the address provided the idea: Am Felsennelkenanger means "At the Proliferous-Pink Meadow." During the Middle Ages, precisely this proliferous pink flower was used to extract pigment for the red coloring of lettering ornamentation. The architects of bogevischs office have reflected this in the design of the façade by attaching the powder-coated metal panels in the façade design with seven different shades of red as protection against the sun. The contemporary ornament decorates the long façade in this manner, and the moveable elements provide a rhythm that offers variety. The planners break up the large structural shell on the interior with a courtyard. The circumferential galleries that lead to the rooms allow views across the floors.

Bei der Münchener Studentenwohnanlage ist die Adresse Ideenlieferant: Am Felsennelkenanger. Im Mittelalter diente die besagte Felsennelke zur Pigmentgewinnung für die Rotfärbung von Schriftverzierungen durch Ornamente. Dies greifen die Architekten von bogevischs buero in der Fassadengestaltung auf, indem sie pulverbeschichtete Metalltafeln in sieben verschiedenen Rottönen als Sonnenschutz anbringen. Das zeitgenössische Ornament verziert so die lange Fassade, und die verschiebbaren Elemente sorgen für einen Rhythmus, der Abwechslung bietet. Den großen Baukörper lösen die Planer innen durch einen Hof auf. Die umlaufenden Galerien, die zu den Zimmern führen, lassen Blickbeziehungen über die Geschosse zu.

En esta residencia de estudiantes muniquesa, la misma dirección ha servido de inspiración: "Felsennelkenanger" vendría a ser un prado de claveles de roca. En la Edad Media se utilizaba esta flor para obtener un pigmento rojo con el que ribetear ornamentos. Los arquitectos de bogevischs buero adoptaron la idea para la fachada, configurada por planchas metálicas con capa pulverizada a modo de protectores solares y en siete tonos diferentes de rojo. La ornamentación contemporánea decora la extensa fachada, mientras que los elementos móviles le proporcionan ritmo y variedad. Los diseñadores dispusieron los grandes volúmenes del interior en un patio circundado por galerías que conducen a las estancias. Estas galerías permiten divisar las diferentes plantas del edificio.

Pour le dortoir des étudiants de Munich, l'adresse a fourni l'idée : Am Felsennelkenanger signifie « A la praire de l'œillet prolifère ». Pendant le Moyen-Age, c'était précisément de cette fleur rose qu'était extrait le pigment pour la coloration rouge des ornementations. Les architectes du bureau Bogevischs l'ont interprété dans le design de la façade en attachant des panneaux de métal couverts de poudre de sept nuances différentes de rouge, servant de protection contre le soleil. Les ornements contemporains décorent ainsi la longue façade, et les éléments mobiles fournissent un rythme offrant une certaine variété. Les concepteurs ont brisé la large coque structurelle de l'intérieur avec une cour intérieure. Les galeries périphériques menant aux chambres permettent une vue à travers les étages.

Alla Münchener Studentenwohnanlage (complesso residenziale per studenti a Monaco) l'indirizzo è fornitore di idee: "Am Felsennelkenanger" (presso lo spazio erboso dei garofani di roccia). Nel medioevo il citato garofano di roccia serviva per l'estrazione dei pigmenti per il colore rosso degli ornamenti della scrittura. Questo dettaglio viene ripreso dagli architetti della bogevischs buero nella strutturazione della facciata, che fissano delle tavole di metallo rivestite in polvere con sette diversi toni di rosso come protezione contro il sole. L'ornamento dell'epoca decora così la lunga facciata e gli elementi spostabili creano un ritmo che offre della varietà. Il grande corpo dell'edificio viene disciolto all'interno dai progettisti tramite un cortile. Le gallerie che corrono tutte intorno e che portano alle camere concedono un rapporto visivo attraverso i piani.

CARLOS MARTINEZ ARCHITEKTEN | WIDNAU, SWITZERLAND
PIPILOTTI RIST, ARTIST | ZURICH, SWITZERLAND

Website	www.carlosmartinez.ch
Website	www.pipilottirist.net
Project	Citylounge St.Gallen
Location	St. Gallen, Switzerland
Year of Completion	2004
Building Materials	Substructure: glass-fiber reinforced plastic (GRP), concrete, granulated rubber; Lounge furniture: substructure of concrete and fiber-glass reinforced plastics
Color specifications	Red granulated rubber, maidenhair-trees for natural green in summer and yellow in autumn
Photo Credits	Hannes Thalmann, Marc Wetli, Till Hückels

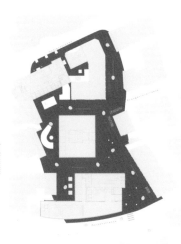

The red floor covering of rubber granulate distinguishes the City Lounge and covers the square, as well as all of the furniture provided in the open space. The "red carpet" even carries the idea of the lounge into the building façades and lets them look like the interior walls of the lounge. As a result, the perception of the interior and exterior space is reversed. All of the furnishing elements develop as free forms from the carpet covering. At the same time, the pleasantly soft haptic contrasts to the hard precision of the structural surroundings. Oversized, amorphous sources of illumination create the necessary and scenic light within the quarter. Stretched across to square on steel ropes, the light sculptures form the upper limits of the space.

Der rote Bodenbelag aus Gummigranulat kennzeichnet die Stadtlounge und überzieht den Platz sowie alle Möbel, die den Freiraum ausstatten. Der „rote Teppich" trägt die Idee der Lounge bis an die Gebäudefassaden und lässt diese als Innenwände der Lounge erscheinen. Die Wahrnehmung von Innen- und Außenraum wird dadurch umgekehrt. Alle Möblierungselemente entwickeln sich als freie Formen aus dem Teppichbelag. Die angenehm weiche Haptik tritt dabei in Kontrast zur harten Präzision der baulichen Umgebung. Überdimensionierte amorphe Leuchtkörper erzeugen sowohl das notwendige, als auch das szenische Licht innerhalb des Quartiers. An den Stahlseilen über den Platz gespannt, begrenzen die Lichtskulpturen den Raum nach oben.

El revestimiento del suelo de granulado de goma rojo caracteriza el Stadtlounge, cubriendo toda la plaza y el mobiliario que decora los espacios exteriores. La "alfombra roja" transporta la idea de este lounge hasta las propias fachadas de los edificios convirtiéndose en sus paredes internas. La percepción del interior y el exterior es la inversa. Todos los elementos del mobiliario son formas abstractas derivadas del propio pavimento. El delicado tacto contrasta con la sólida precisión del entorno edificado. Unas inmensas esculturas lumínicas de forma irregular aportan la luz necesaria al complejo, dándole igualmente un toque efectista. Suspendidas en unos cables de acero que cruzan la plaza, sirven de linde aérea a este espacio.

Le revêtement de sol en granulés rouge caractérise le City Lounge et recouvre à la fois le square et les meubles disposés à l'air libre. Le « tapis rouge » apporte même l'idée de la salle de séjour au niveau des façades de l'immeuble : elles paraissent être les murs intérieurs du lounge. Ainsi, la perception des espaces intérieur et extérieur est inversée. Tous les éléments du mobilier se développent comme des formes libres à partir du revêtement. Parallèlement, l'agréable douceur haptique contraste avec la précision dure des structures environnantes. Des sources de lumière démesurées, amorphes, créent l'éclairage scénique nécessaire dans le quartier. Etirées à travers le square sur des cordes d'acier, les sculptures de lumière forment les limites supérieures de l'espace.

Il rivestimento del pavimento rosso in granulato di gomma caratterizza la Stadtlounge e riveste la piazza e tutti i mobili, che arredano lo spazio all'area aperta. Il "tappeto rosso" trasporta l'idea della lounge fino alle facciate degli edifici e le fa apparire come le pareti interne della lounge. La percezione dello spazio interno e dello spazio esterno viene così capovolta. Tutti gli elementi della mobilia si sviluppano come forme libere che fuoriescono dal rivestimento del tappeto. Il tocco morbido e piacevole si pone così in contrasto con la dura precisione dell'ambiente costruttivo. Delle illuminazioni di grandezza eccezionale generano sia la luce necessaria sia la luce scenica all'interno del quartiere. Tramite delle funi d'acciaio, che sono state tirate sulla piazza, queste sculture di luce delimitano lo spazio verso l'alto.

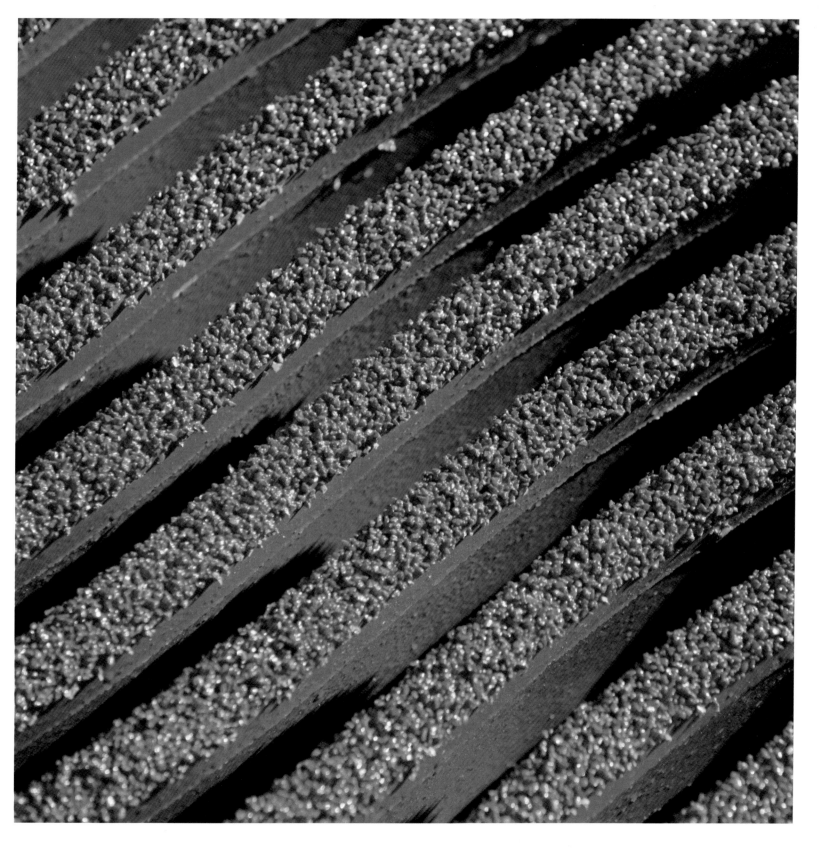

CODE UNIQUE ARCHITEKTEN | DRESDEN, GERMANY
ARCHITEKTENGEMEINSCHAFT ZIMMERMANN | DRESDEN, GERMANY

Website	www.codeunique.de
	www.ag-zimmermann.de
Project	Computing Faculty of TU Dresden
Location	Dresden, Germany
Year of Completion	2006
Building Materials	Reinforced concrete, fiber cement, colored glass, aluminum (panels or expanded metal), rubber and textile coverings, epoxy resin coating with variable treatment of surface textures and colors, depending on use
Color specification	Natural rubber and fitted carpeting, epoxy coating, paint
Photo Credits	Courtesy of AG Zimmermann + Code Unique

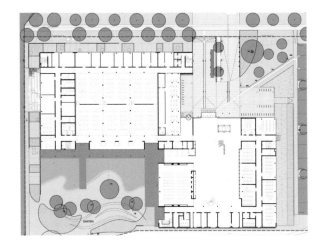

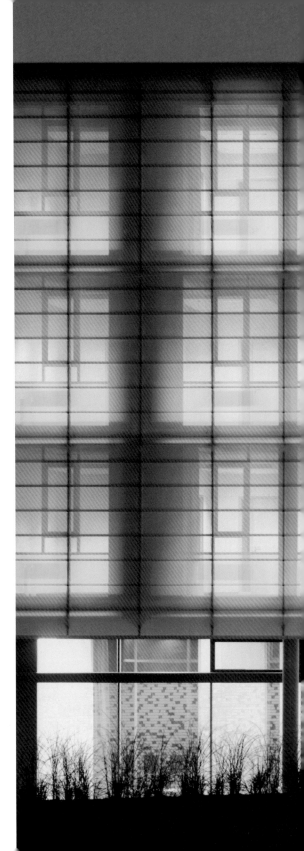

With the new building of the Faculty of Informatics at the Technical University of Dresden, the architect team of Zimmermann and Code Unique Architekten has set urban-developmental and architectural accents in the heterogeneous surroundings of the western part of Dresden's Südstadt. Closed in the direction of Nöthnitzer Strasse, the albeit strict structural shell forms various open and inner-courtyard spaces through its meandering shape, which creates room for communication. The architects play with contrasts such as exterior and interior, exposed concrete and glass. The green reflects the experimental character of the teaching and research activities. Eyes that are fatigued because of the screen realities can recover quickly here.

Avec le nouveau bâtiment de la Faculté d'informatique de l'Université Technique de Dresde, l'équipe d'architectes de Zimmermann and Code Unique Architekten a apporté une touche d'architecture et de développement urbain à l'environnement hétérogène du sud-ouest de Dresde. Fermée dans la direction de la Nöthnitzer Strasse, la stricte coque structurelle forme pourtant divers espaces ouverts et cours intérieures grâce à sa forme sinueuse, qui crée un espace pour la communication. Les architectes jouent avec les contrastes : intérieur et extérieur, béton apparent et verre. Le vert reflète le caractère expérimental des activités d'enseignement et de recherche. Les yeux fatigués par les écrans peuvent facilement récupérer ici.

Mit dem Neubau der Fakultät Informatik der Technischen Universität Dresden setzen die Architektengemeinschaft Zimmermann und Code Unique Architekten einen städtebaulichen und architektonischen Akzent in dem heterogenen Umfeld in der westlichen Südstadt. Zur Nöthnitzer Straße hin geschlossen, formt der an sich strikte Baukörper durch seine Mäanderform unterschiedliche Frei- und Innenhofflächen und schafft Raum für Kommunikation. Die Architekten spielen mit Kontrasten wie Außen und Innen, Sichtbeton und Glas. Das Grün spiegelt den experimentellen Charakter des Lehr- und Forschungsbetriebes wider. Von den Bildschirmrealitäten ermüdete Augen erholen sich hier schnell.

Con il nuovo edificio della Facoltà di Informatica della Università Tecnica di Dresda l'associazione di architetti Zimmermann e gli architetti Code Unique hanno posto un accento urbanistico e architettonico nell'ambiente eterogeneo nella parte occidentale del sud della città. Chiuso verso la Nöthnitzer Straße, il corpo dell'edificio, che di per sé è rigoroso, forma grazie alla sua forma a meandro varie aree all'aperto e per cortili interni, e crea dei luoghi per la comunicazione. Gli architetti giocano con i contrasti come fuori e dentro, cemento a vista e vetro. Il verde rispecchia il carattere sperimentale dell'esercizio formativo e dell'attività di ricerca. Gli occhi stanchi a causa dai monitor si possono riprendere rapidamente qui.

Con la nueva Facultad de Informática de la Universidad Técnica de Dresde (Alemania), el colectivo de arquitectos Zimmerman y los arquitectos de Code Unique le han dado un toque urbano y arquitectónico a un entorno tan heterogéneo como es el de esta ciudad del este de Alemania. Enmarcada en la calle Nöthnitzer y mediante su forma semejante a meandros, esta construcción de líneas estrictas crea superficies abiertas y patios que fomentan la comunicación. Los arquitectos juegan con contrastes como interior-exterior u hormigón cara vista-cristal. El verde refleja el carácter experimental de este centro de enseñanza e investigación, en el que los ojos cansados ante la realidad de las pantallas encuentran rápido alivio.

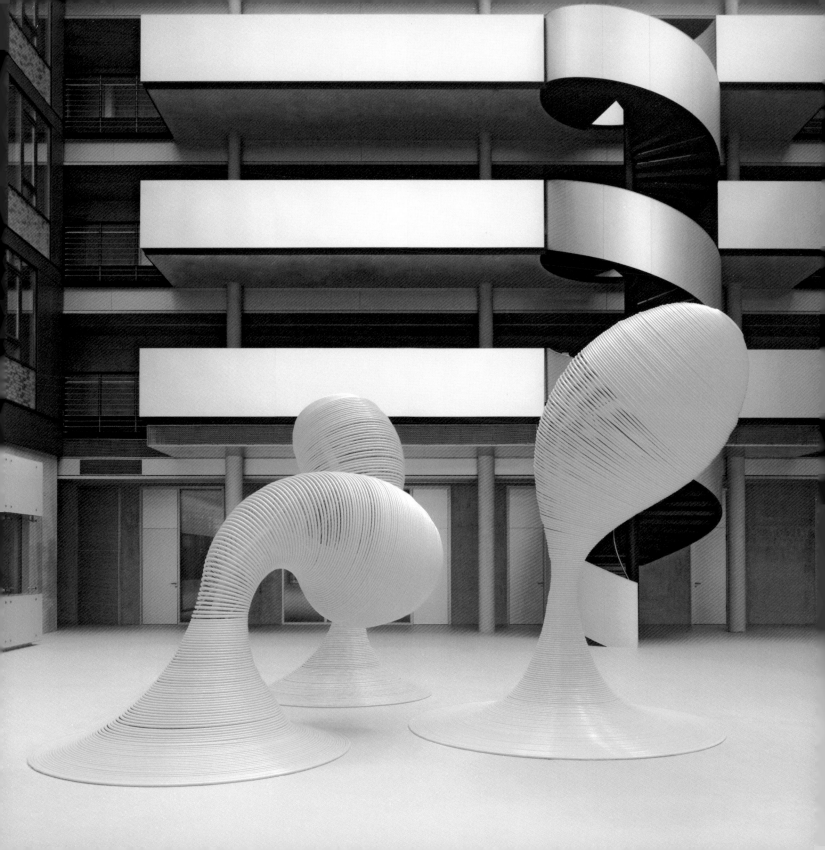

COLLABORATIVE ARCHITECTURE | MUMBAI, INDIA

Website	www.collaborativearchitecture.com
Project	Concept Pavilion for Titan Industries
Location	Mobile (First Installation at Delhi, India)
Year of Completion	2006
Building Materials	Stands made of flexi-ply on mild steel frames, plexiglass display units
Color specifications	Acrylic paint in red, white
Photo Credits	Lalita Tharani

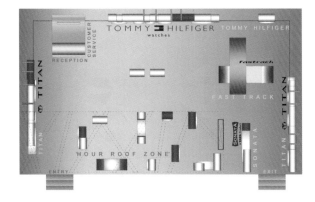

This exhibition pavilion portrays the presence and sense of time. The largest manufacturer in India wanted a pavilion reflecting the future direction of the company and showcasing the various brands they represent. The team of Collaborative Architecture unified these directions as Time Zones, with the Subzones representing different brands. With the Hour Roof, the architects suggest radically different coordinates for the definition of "space". "Time", as the fourth dimensional theoretical construct, forms a tangible spatial index. The company color of red dominates the color scheme.

Ein Ausstellungspavillon ganz im Zeichen der Zeit. Der größte Uhrenhersteller Indiens wünschte einen Pavillon, der die Zukunftsausrichtung widerspiegelt und die unterschiedlichen Marken des Unternehmens präsentiert. Das Team von Collaborative Archtitecture vereint die Anforderungen – wörtlich – unter einem Dach: unter dem „Dach der Stunde" findet sich die „Zeitzone", die sich in die einzelnen Ausstellungsflächen für die Marken, in die „Subzonen", unterteilt. Mit dem Pavillon schlagen die Architekten andere Koordinaten für die Definition „Raum" vor: Die Zeit als vierte Dimension und theoretisches Konstrukt bildet einen fühlbaren, räumlichen Index. Rot, die Unternehmensfarbe, bestimmt die Farbgebung.

Este pabellón de exposición transmite la presencia y el sentido del tiempo. El mayor fabricante de relojes de la India buscaba un pabellón que reflejara su orientación hacia el futuro y en el que estuvieran representadas sus diferentes marcas. La respuesta del equipo de Collaborative Archtitecture fue la unificación por "zonas horarias", donde las "subzonas" representaban diferentes marcas. Con el "Techo de la hora", los arquitectos propusieron unas coordenadas radicalmente diferentes para definir el "espacio". El "tiempo", cuarta dimensión y constructo teórico, establece un registro tangible y espacial. El rojo, el color de la firma, marca la paleta cromática.

Ce pavillon d'exposition dépeint la présence et la signification du temps. Le plus grand fabricant d'Inde voulait un pavillon reflétant la direction future de l'entreprise et exposant les différentes marques qu'elle représente. L'équipe de Collaborative Architecture a suivi ces directives en créant des Zones Temps où des Sous-zones représentent différentes marques. Avec le Toit de l'Heure, les architectes proposent des coordonnées radicalement différentes pour la définition de « l'espace ». Le « temps », en tant que quatrième dimension et concept théorique, forme un indice spatial tangible. Le rouge, couleur de l'entreprise, domine l'agencement des couleurs.

Un padiglione della mostra completamente nei segni dei tempi. Il più grande produttore di orologi dell'India ha desiderato avere un padiglione che rifletta l'orientamento per il futuro e che possa presentare i marchi dell'impresa. La squadra di Collaborative Archtitecture ha unito le richieste – in senso letterario – sotto un unico tetto: sotto il "tetto dell'ora" si trova il "fuso orario" che si suddivide nelle singole superfici della mostra per i marchi, nelle "sottozone". Con questo padiglione gli architetti suggeriscono altre coordinate per la definizione di "spazio": il tempo come quarta dimensione e costruzione teorica forma un indice che può essere sentito e che riguarda lo spazio. Il rosso, il colore dell'azienda, decide la scelta del colore.

COLLABORATIVE ARCHITECTURE | MUMBAI, INDIA

Website	www.collaborativearchitecture.com
Project	Wrap-3
Project website	www.jdtislam.org
Location	JDT Orphanage, Calicut, Kerala, India
Year of Completion	2006
Building Materials	Mild steel frame clad with plywood and laminate
Color specifications	Green, violet and blue laminate, gypsum board ceiling finished in acrylic paint
Photo Credits	Ajeeb Komachi, Lalita Tharani

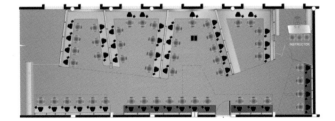

In an orphanage in Calcutta, India, children look forward to returning to their computer classes. The training center designed by Collaborative Architecture sparkles with dynamism and a celebration of color. Organic forms float through the area of 1800 sq. ft. and divide the learning space into individual domains. The counters are suspended from the ceiling and leave the floor free of visible supports, creating the impression of floating space. The doodles by the youngsters were the architects' inspiration for the cutouts in the "wraps." The colors green, violet, and blue generate overlapping and continuously changing spatial compositions with each vantage point offering a variety of discoveries.

In einem Waisenhaus in Kalkutta in Indien freuen sich Kinder darauf, wieder den Computer-Unterricht aufnehmen zu dürfen. Das Ausbildungszentrum, das vom Collaborative Architecture-Team entworfen wurde, sprüht vor Dynamik und Farbenfreude. Organische Formen schweben über die Fläche von mehr als 160 m² und unterteilen den Raum in einzelne Arbeitsbereiche. Die Einbauten wurden an der Decke aufgehängt, so dass der Boden frei von sichtbaren Auflagen ist, wodurch der Eindruck eines schwebenden Raumes entsteht. Das Gekritzel der Kinder inspirierte die Planer für die Ausschnitte in den „Wraps". Die Farben Grün, Violett und Blau generieren Überlappungen und je nach Blickwinkel ständig wechselnde räumliche Kompositionen, so dass der Raum vielfältige Entdeckungen bietet.

Los niños de un orfanato de la ciudad de Calcuta en India están deseando volver a las clases de informática. El centro de formación diseñado por Collaborative Architecture destila dinamismo y es una explosión de color. Unas formas orgánicas suspendidas sobre una superficie de más de 160 m² dividen el espacio en diferentes áreas. Los elementos cuelgan del techo y el suelo queda así libre de soportes, consiguiéndose una sensación de "espacio flotante". Los garabatos de los niños sirvieron de inspiración para diseñar las piezas de este "envoltorio". El verde, el violeta y el azul se superponen modificando continuamente la composición espacial: cada perspectiva es un nuevo descubrimiento.

Dans un orphelinat de Calcutta, en Inde, les enfants ont hâte de retourner en cours d'informatique. Le centre de formation qu'a conçu Collaborative Architecture pétille de dynamisme et célèbre la couleur. Des formes organiques flottent à travers une surface de 160 m² et divisent l'espace d'apprentissage en domaines individuels. Les comptoirs sont suspendus au plafond et laissent le sol libre de tout support visible, créant une impression d'espace flottant. Les gribouillages des enfants ont inspiré les architectes pour les découpes des « wraps ». Les couleurs vert, violet et bleu génèrent des compositions qui se chevauchent et changent continuellement selon chaque point de vue, offrant une variété de découvertes.

In un orfanotrofio a Calcutta, in India, i bambini sono felici di poter tornare alle loro lezioni di computer. Le sale formazione, che sono state elaborate dalla squadra della Collaborative Architecture, sfavillano di dinamicità e di una celebrazione di colori. Delle forme organiche si liberano attraverso la superficie di più di 160 m² e suddividono lo spazio per studiare in locali individuali. I banchi sono appesi dal soffitto, lasciando così il pavimento libero da supporti visibili e creando uno "spazio galleggiante nell'aria". Gli scarabocchi dei bambini hanno ispirato i progettisti per i ritagli nelle "Wraps". I colori verde, viola e blu generano delle sovrapposizioni e composizioni dello spazio che cambiano costantemente con ogni punto di vista, offrendo così una molteplicità di scoperte.

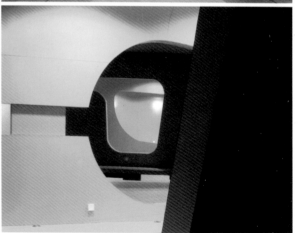

DAIGO ISHII + FUTURE-SCAPE ARCHITECTS | TOKYO, JAPAN

Website   www.future-scape.co.jp
Project   White Blue Black
Location   Mitaka, Tokyo, Japan
Year of Completion   1997
Building Materials   Reinforced concrete construction, steel, plywood
Color Specifications Concrete painted with exterior type of acrylic emulsion,
                     lumber-core plywood painted with acrylic, homegenous
                     vinyl tile, galvanized steel finished in exterior-type oil
                     paint, oil-painted steel, plywood painted with oil stain
Photo Credits   Japan Architects (p 133), Daigo Ishii + Future-scape
                     Architects

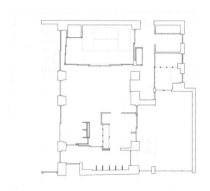

The residential building for a book-lover was designed according to a simple rule: The structure of the house is in white, the supportive elements in black, and all of the bookshelves are kept in blue. Blue is a color, according to the Future-scape Architects, that does not unite with the "existence of the books" and therefore erases the heaviness of the books. This color rule determines the appearance of the interior. The bookshelves do not just surround the rooms but also serve as passageways. When the doors are open, all of the bookshelves are connected with each other; when the doors are closed, they become a buffer zone between the rooms. The shelves also serve as a channel for natural daylight in the vertical direction.

Das Wohnhaus für einen Buchliebhaber gestaltet sich nach einer simplen Regel: Die Struktur des Hauses ist in weiß, tragende Elemente in schwarz und sämtliche Bücherregale sind in blau gehalten. Blau sei eine Farbe, so die Future-scape Architects, die sich nicht mit der „Existenz der Bücher" vereine und dadurch die Schwere der Bücher ausradiere. Diese Farbregel bestimmt das Aussehen des Interieurs. Die Bücherregale umrunden nicht einfach die Räume, sondern dienen als Passagen. Bei geöffneten Türen stehen alle Bücherregale in Verbindung, bei geschlossenen Türen werden sie zur Pufferzone zwischen den Räumen. Auch in vertikale Richtung dienen die Regale als eine Passage für das natürliche Tageslicht.

Esta construcción residencial para un amante de los libros se diseñó siguiendo una regla muy sencilla: la estructura de la casa va en blanco, los elementos portantes en negro y las estanterías para libros en azul. Según los arquitectos de Future-scape, el azul es un color que no encaja con la "existencia de libros"; por lo que elimina el peso de los mismos. Estas reglas cromáticas determinan el aspecto interior. Las estanterías no solo rodean las estancias, sino que sirven de pasillo. Con las puertas abiertas, se ve cómo todas las estanterías conectan unas con otras. Con las puertas cerradas, hacen de tope entre las estancias. En sentido vertical, las estanterías sirven también de corredor de la luz natural.

Cette résidence d'un bibliophile a été conçue selon une règle simple : la structure de la maison est blanche, les éléments de soutien sont noirs, et toutes les bibliothèques sont bleues. Le bleu est une couleur qui, selon les architectes de Future-scape, ne s'unit pas avec « l'existence des livres » et efface donc la lourdeur des livres. Cette règle de couleur détermine l'apparence de l'intérieur. Les bibliothèques n'entourent pas seulement les pièces mais servent aussi de voies de passage. Quand les portes sont ouvertes, toutes les bibliothèques sont connectées entre elles ; quand les portes sont fermées, elles forment une zone tampon entre les pièces. Les étagères servent aussi de vecteur pour la lumière naturelle dans le sens vertical.

La casa per un amante di libri è stata strutturata secondo una semplice regola: La struttura della casa è bianca, gli elementi portanti sono neri e tutti gli scaffali per libri sono dipinti di blu. Il blu sarebbe un colore, secondo i Future-scape Architects, che non si unisce con la "esistenza dei libri" e quindi cancella il peso dei libri. Questa regola di colore definisce l'aspetto degli interni. Gli scaffali per libri non hanno solamente la funzione di circondare semplicemente le stanze, ma servono da passaggi. Quando le porte sono aperte tutti gli scaffali per libri sono collegati tra loro, quando le porte sono chiuse diventano delle zone cuscinetto tra le stanze. Gli scaffali servono anche in direzione verticale come passaggi per la luce naturale del giorno.

DORTE MANDRUP ARCHITECTS | COPENHAGEN, DENMARK

Website	www.dortemandrup.dk
Project	Day-Care Centre Skanderborggade
Location	Skanderborggade, Copenhagen, Denmark
Year of Completion	2005
Building Materials	Concrete components, slope made of plywood, façade of stained pinewood frames and silk-screened glass
Color Specifications	Interior: red linoleum, upper garden with red, green, blue, yellow granulated rubber
Photo Credits	Jens Markus Lindhe

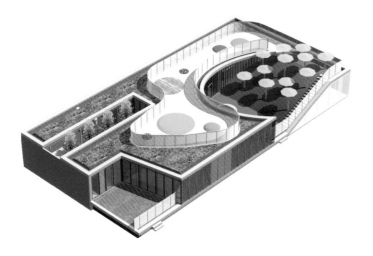

The regulations only allowed for one floor so that the good lighting of the five-story neighbor building from the 19th century and its inner courtyards would not be jeopardized. The Dorte Mandrup Architects skillfully circumvented this restriction so that the children in the Day-Care Center of Copenhagen are allowed to climb on the roof to play. However, this is not a surface separated from the building. The planners created a slope that connects the roof with the play area on the ground-floor level. A space for play even during rainy weather is located beneath it—they can swing between the supporting concrete pillars. The roof garden and courtyard are covered with red rubber granulate; the hills on them are green, blue, and yellow.

Die Vorschriften sahen nur ein Geschoss vor, um eine gute Belichtung der fünfgeschossigen Nachbarbebauung aus dem 19. Jahrhundert und ihrer Innenhöfe nicht zu gefährden. Die Dorte Mandrup Architects umgehen diese Einschränkung geschickt, so dass die Kinder in dem Day-Care Center in Kopenhagen zum Spielen aufs Dach steigen dürfen. Das ist aber keine vom Gebäude abgetrennte Fläche, sondern die Planer schaffen einen Hang, der das Dach mit der Spielfläche auf Erdgeschoss-Ebene verbindet. Darunter ergibt sich eine Fläche zum Spielen selbst bei Regen – zwischen den tragenden Betonsäulen wird geschaukelt. Der Dachgarten und der Hof sind mit rotem Gummi-Granulat belegt, die Hügel darin sind grün, blau und gelb.

La normativa prevé una única planta para no restar luminosidad a las cinco alturas de los edificios colindantes del siglo XIX ni a sus patios interiores. Los arquitectos de Dorte Mandrup supieron salvar esta limitación de forma inteligente para que los niños de esta guardería de Copenhague pudieran acceder al tejado para jugar. Sin embargo, el tejado no es una superficie ajena al edificio. Los diseñadores crearon una rampa que comunicaba el tejado con la zona de juego de la planta baja. De este modo se creó incluso una zona de juego para días lluviosos, ya que pueden columpiarse entre los pilares de hormigón. El jardín del tejado y el patio están cubiertos con goma granulada de color rojo. Las colinas son verdes, azules y amarillas.

Il n'était autorisé de construire qu'un seul étage pour que l'ensoleillement des cinq étages et de la cour intérieure du bâtiment voisin, datant du XIXème siècle, n'aient pas à en pâtir. Les architectes de Dorte Mandrup Architects ont habilement contourné cette restriction pour que les enfants du Centre de Jour de Copenhague soient autorisés à monter sur le toit pour jouer. Cependant, ce n'est pas une surface séparée du reste du bâtiment. Les concepteurs ont créé une pente qui relie le toit à la salle de jeu du rez-de-chaussée. Un espace pour jouer même lorsqu'il pleut est situé en dessous – les enfants peuvent se balancer entre les piliers de soutènement en béton. Le jardin et la cour du toit sont couverts de granulés de caoutchouc rouge, avec des protubérances vertes, bleues et jaunes.

Le disposizioni prevedevano solo un piano, per non mettere a repentaglio la buona illuminazione della costruzione adiacente di cinque piani del 19. secolo e dei suoi cortili interni. Gli architetti della Dorte Mandrup hanno ovviato a queste limitazioni con abilità, così che i bambini del Cay-Care Center a Copenaghen possono andare a giocare sul tetto. Questo però non è una superficie separata dall'edificio, ma i progettisti hanno creato un pendio che collega il tetto con l'area giochi sul livello al pian terreno. Sotto si viene a creare una superficie per giocare anche quando piove – tra le colonne in cemento portanti si può andare in altalena. Il giardino pensile e il cortile sono rivestiti di granulato di gomma rosso, le colline al loro interno sono verdi, blu e gialle.

DORTE MANDRUP ARCHITECTS | COPENHAGEN, DENMARK
WITH B&K+ BRANDLHUBER & CO. | BERLIN, GERMANY

Website	www.dortemandrup.dk
	www.brandlhuber.com
Project	Sports and Culture Centre: Crystal
Location	Holmbladsgade, Copenhagen, Denmark
Year of Completion	2006
Building Materials	Steel and timber structure covered with opalescent poly-carbonate panels
Color Specifications	Green polyurethane sports flooring, end walls of painted concrete
Photo Credits	Torben Eskerod

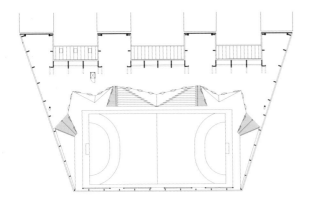

The derivation of the design is practical: Four existing gable walls of the neighboring structures and the large volume required by a hall for ball sports are the determining factors. The shell of the building connects the set points. The team of Dorte Mandrup Architects and b&k+ brandlhuber selected translucent polycarbonate panels that do not let any direct sunlight pass through and therefore provide anti-glare daylight conditions as the material for the shell. Sports are played on a "lawn"—so green is appropriate. This is supplemented by the supporting structure of steel and wood, providing an almost natural atmosphere. The hall is illuminated in the evening, allowing the green to shimmer through it to the outside.

Die Herleitung des Entwurfs ist praktisch: Vier bestehende Giebelwände der Nachbarbebauung und das große Volumen, das eine Halle für Ballsportarten erfordert, sind bestimmende Faktoren. Die Gebäudehülle verbindet die vorgegebenen Punkte. Als Material für die Hülle wählen das Team von den Dorte Mandrup Architects und von b&k+ brandlhuber transluzente Polycarbonat-Stegplatten, die kein direktes Sonnenlicht durchlassen und somit für blendfreie Tageslichtbedingungen sorgen. Sport wird auf einer „Rasenfläche" getrieben – Grün ist angesagt. Das ergänzt sich mit dem Tragwerk aus Stahl und Holz und sorgt für eine fast natürliche Atmosphäre. Abends leuchtet die Halle und das Grün schimmert nach außen hin durch.

Los factores determinantes de los que deriva el diseño son de lo más práctico: cuatro frontones existentes de las edificaciones adyacentes y un gran volumen que debe albergar un pabellón para deportes con balón. El cubrimiento del edificio conecta los puntos dados. Los arquitectos de Dorte Mandrup y b&k + brandlhuber eligieron para este cubrimiento unas planchas de policarbonato translúcido que no dejan pasar la luz directa, así que la luz natural que llega no deslumbra. Los deportes se practican en una superficie de "hierba", por lo que su color es el verde. La estructura portante de acero y madera sirve de complemento y crea un ambiente de lo más natural. Con la iluminación nocturna, el verde resplandece en el exterior del pabellón.

L'origine du design est pratique : les quatre murs pignon existants des structures voisines et le large volume nécessaire à une salle de sports de balle ont été les facteurs déterminants. La coque du bâtiment relie les points fixes. L'équipe de Dorte Mandrup Architects et b&k + brandhulber a choisi comme matériau pour la coque des panneaux de polycarbonate transparent qui ne laissent passer aucune lumière directe et fournissent ainsi une protection anti-éblouissement. Les sports sont pratiqués sur une « pelouse » – le vert est donc approprié. Grâce à la structure de soutien en bois et acier, l'atmosphère est quasiment naturelle. La salle est illuminée le soir, ce qui permet au vert de briller vers l'extérieur.

La derivazione del progetto è pratica: quattro pareti già esistenti della costruzione adiacente, culminanti in forma cuspidale, e il grande volume richiesto dalla palestra per attività sportive con la palla, sono dei fattori decisivi. L'involucro dell'edificio collega i punti prestabiliti. Il materiale dell'involucro scelto dalla squadra degli architetti della Dörte Mandrup e della b&k+ brandlhuber sono state delle piastre traslucide in policarbonato, che non consentono un passaggio diretto della luce del sole e creano così delle condizioni di luce del giorno antiabbagliante. Lo sport si pratica su una "superficie erbosa" – il verde si impone. Quest'ultimo si integra con la struttura portante di acciaio e legno e crea un'atmosfera quasi naturale. La sera la palestra e il verde risplendono dall'interno verso l'esterno.

FRIIS & MOLTKE I ÅRHUS, AALBORG, KØGE, DENMARK

Website	www.friis-moltke.dk
Project	Lundskolen School
Location	Horsens, Denmark
Year of Completion	2007
Building Materials	Lightweight glass façades with concrete base
Color Specifications	Colored enameled glass, red, orange and yellow laminate, painted walls
Photo Credits	Courtesy of Friis & Moltke, Århus and Anders Brohus

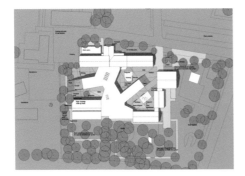

With the enlargement of the Lundskolen, the architects Friis & Moltke have given the school a new heart. An artist designed the 115-foot long exposed-concrete wall that allows art and architecture to interact. The space expands across two floors that are connected by a staircase. Wall surfaces are primarily white; individual areas, corridors as well as doors, are kept in a dark, hardwearing gray. The planners used colors to set accents, such as red room dividers and niches. Changes of color in the floors mark walking lines and transitions. The light glass façade, which stands on a concrete base, creates the impression of a mosaic because it is broken up by the color enameled glass surfaces.

Mit der Erweiterung der Lundskolen haben die Architekten Friis & Moltke der Schule ein neues Herz verliehen. Ein Künstler gestaltete die 35 m lange Sichtbetonwand und lässt Kunst und Architektur zusammen wirken. Der Raum öffnet sich über zwei Etagen, die eine Treppe verbindet. Wandflächen sind überwiegend weiß, einzelne Bereiche, Korridore sowie Türen sind in dunklem, unempfindlichem Grau gehalten. Mit Farben setzen die Planer Akzente, etwa durch rote Raumteiler und Nischen. Farbwechsel in den Fußböden markieren Lauflinien und Übergänge. In der leichten Glasfassade, die auf einem Betonsockel steht, entsteht ein Eindruck von einem Mosaik durch die Auflockerung durch farbig emaillierte Glasflächen.

Con la ampliación del colegio de Lundskolen, los arquitectos Friis & Moltke le han dado un nuevo corazón. Un artista diseñó la pared de 35 m de largo de hormigón cara vista que permite interactuar arte con arquitectura. El espacio se extiende por dos plantas unidas por una escalera. Las paredes son en su mayoría blancas, mientras que algunas áreas, los pasillos y las puertas son de un gris oscuro neutral. Los colores les sirven a los planificadores para marcar diferencias, como los separadores y nichos rojos. Los diferentes colores en el pavimento marcan líneas de paso y transiciones. La liviana fachada de cristal, apoyada en un zócalo de hormigón, parece más un mosaico gracias a las divisiones creadas por los cristales esmaltados en color.

En agrandissant Lundskolen, les architectes Friis & Moltke ont donné un nouveau cœur à l'école. Un artiste a conçu le mur de béton apparent de 35 m de long qui permet une interaction entre l'art et à l'architecture. Les espaces s'étendent à travers les deux niveaux connectés par un escalier. Les surfaces murales sont d'abord blanches ; des zones particulières, les couloirs et les portes, restent d'un gris foncé robuste. Les concepteurs ont utilisé les couleurs pour donner le ton, par exemple avec des cloisons et des niches rouges. Les changements de couleur des sols indiquent les lignes de circulation et les transitions. La façade en verre léger, posée sur une base en béton, a l'apparence d'une mosaïque parce que cassée par les surfaces en verre de couleur émaillé.

Con l'ampliamento delle Lundskolen gli architetti Friis & Moltke hanno dato alla scuola un nuovo cuore. Un artista ha dato forma ai 35 m del muro in calcestruzzo a vista e ha fatto agire insieme l'arte e l'architettura. Lo spazio si apre su due piani, uniti da una scala. Le pareti sono prevalentemente bianche, delle singole aree, corridoi e porte sono tenute in un grigio scuro e resistente. Con dei colori i progettisti hanno posto degli accenti, per esempio con divisori e nicchie rossi. Delle variazioni nel colore dei pavimenti segnano le linee dei percorsi e i passaggi. Nelle leggere facciate di vetro che sono installate su un basamento in calcestruzzo, si crea l'impressione di un mosaico grazie allo scioglimento tramite superfici colorate di vetro smaltato.

JOHNSEN SCHMALING ARCHITECTS | MILWAUKEE (WI), USA

Website	www.johnsenschmaling.com
Project	Camouflage House
Location	Green Lake (WI), USA
Year of Completion	2006
Building Materials	Concrete, cedar, engineered wood, Prodema wood veneer panels, glass, MDF
Color Specifications	Cedar and colored wood veneer panels
Photo Credits	John J. Macaulay Photography, Kevin Miyazaki, Milwaukee (WI)

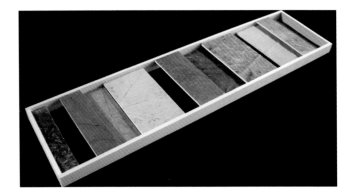

The **Camouflage House disguises** itself on the steep banks of a lake in Milwaukee. Only a rough driveway leads to the silhouette that disappears under the trees. With its simple ground plan and a reduced use of materials, the residential building attains clarity while radiating a warm atmosphere. Johnsen Schmaling Architects divided the horizontal façade into vertical wood and window elements that take up the rhythm of the tree trunks. The wood surfaces are layered: The first level consists of untreated cedar wood that shimmers silvery-gray, depending upon the weather influences. The second layer of façade panels reflects the constantly changing hues of nature.

Am Steilufer eines Sees in Milwaukee tarnt sich das Camouflage House. Nur eine raue Zufahrt führt zu der Silhouette, die unter den Bäumen verschwindet. Das Wohnhaus erreicht durch seinen einfachen Grundriss und durch einen reduzierten Materialeinsatz Klarheit, gleichzeitig strahlt es eine warme Atmosphäre aus. Die Johnsen Schmaling Architekten unterteilen die horizontale Fassade in vertikale Holz- und Fensterelemente, die den Rhythmus der Baumstämme aufgreifen. Die Holzflächen schichten sich: Die erste Ebene besteht aus unbehandeltem Zedernholz, das nach Witterungseinfluss silbergrau schimmert. Die zweite Schicht aus Fassadenplatten spiegelt die sich stets ändernden Farbtöne der Natur wider.

La Camouflage House (Casa Camuflaje) se mimetiza en la empinada ribera de un lago en Milwaukee (EE. UU.). Tras conducir por un escarpado camino se distingue su silueta, que desaparece tras la arboleda. Con un plano sencillo y un reducido uso de materiales, consigue claridad de líneas y, al tiempo, un ambiente cálido. Los arquitectos de Johnsen Schmaling dividieron la fachada horizontal con elementos de madera y ventanas dispuestas en vertical para integrarse en el ritmo de los troncos. Las superficies de madera constan de varias capas: la primera es de cedro sin tratar que adquiere unos tonos grisáceoplateados según el efecto de la intemperie. La segunda capa de las planchas de la fachada refleja los siempre cambiantes tonos cromáticos de la naturaleza.

La Camouflage House se déguise sur les pentes raides d'un lac de Milwaukee. Seul un sentier irrégulier mène jusqu'à sa silhouette qui disparaît sous les arbres. Grâce au plan en rez-de-chaussée et à l'utilisation réduite de matériaux, les bâtiments résidentiels gagnent en clarté tout en dégageant une atmosphère chaleureuse. Johnsen Schmaling Architects a divisé la façade horizontale en éléments verticaux de fenêtre et bois qui suivent le rythme des troncs d'arbres. Les surfaces de bois sont superposées : le premier niveau consiste de bois de cèdre non-traité d'un gris argenté qui miroite selon le temps qu'il fait. La seconde couche de panneaux de façade reflète les teintes constamment changeantes de la nature.

Sulla sponda scoscesa di un lago a Milwaukee si mimetizza la Camouflage House. Solo un accesso sterrato conduce alla silhouette che scompare sotto gli alberi. L'abitazione raggiunge chiarezza grazie alla sua semplice pianta e a un utilizzo ridotto di materiale, al contempo irradia una calda atmosfera. Gli architetti della Johnsen Schmaling hanno suddiviso la facciata orizzontale in elementi verticali di legno e di finestre che riprendono il ritmo dei tronchi d'albero. Le superfici in legno si dispongono a strati: il primo livello è costituito da legno di cedro non trattato che dopo l'influsso del tempo risplende in grigioargento. Il secondo strato fatto con lastre di facciata riflette i colori della natura che cambiano costantemente.

JOHNSEN SCHMALING ARCHITECTS | MILWAUKEE (WI), USA

Website   www.johnsenschmaling.com
Project   Parts House Pavilion
Location   Milwaukee (WI), USA
Year of Completion 2004
Building Materials Steel, acrylic plastic, IPE wood
Color Specifications Polychromatic transparent and translucent acrylic plastic
Photo Credits   John J. Macaulay Photography, Milwaukee (WI)

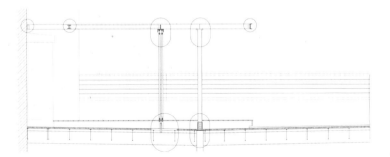

The developer wanted an outdoor living room on the roof of a warehouse from the 1920s, created for intimate dinners—as well as large events—and secluded for a sunbath with a simultaneous view of the city. Johnsen Schmaling Architects proposed a pavilion above the roofs with a "curtain" of moveable steel frames. They intend to use colorful transparent and translucent plastic for the filling. Depending on the position, the elements create various degrees of privacy and immerse the contours of the city in yellow, red, and blue—unaccustomed perspectives. At night, the illuminated pavilion sets an accent in the otherwise dark southern skyline.

Ein Outdoor-Wohnzimmer auf dem Dach eines Warenlagers aus den zwanziger Jahren wünschte der Bauherr, geschaffen sowohl für intime Dinner als auch für große Events, abgeschieden für ein Sonnenbad bei gleichzeitiger Aussicht auf die Stadt. Die Johnsen Schmaling Architekten schlagen einen Pavillon über den Dächern vor mit einem „Vorhang" aus verschiebbaren Stahlrahmen. Für die Füllung sehen sie farbigen transparenten und transluzenten Kunststoff vor. Je nach Position sorgen die Elemente für einen unterschiedlichen Grad an Privatheit, tauchen die Umrisse der Stadt in Gelb, Rot und Blau und sorgen so für ungewohnte Aussichten. Nachts setzt der illuminierte Pavillon einen Akzent in der sonst dunklen südlichen Skyline.

El promotor quería una sala de estar descubierta en la azotea de un antiguo almacén de los años veinte en la que celebrar tanto cenas íntimas como eventos mayores, y que permitiera tomar el sol sin ser visto, pero disfrutando de las vistas sobre la ciudad. La propuesta de los arquitectos de Johnsen Schmaling fue un edificio por encima de los tejados con una "cortina" de marcos de acero movibles, rellenados con material plástico translúcido de diversos colores. Según su posición, estos elementos crean varios grados de privacidad y tiñen el contorno de la ciudad de amarillo, rojo o azul, dando lugar a un panorama muy original. De noche, el pabellón iluminado deja su impronta en la oscuridad de la zona sur de la ciudad.

Le concepteur voulait une salle de séjour extérieure sur le toit d'un entrepôt des années 20, idéale pour des dîners intimes - ainsi que pour des soirées plus importantes - et isolée pour un bain de soleil avec vue sur la ville. Les architectes de Johnsen Schmaling Architects ont proposé un pavillon sur les toits avec un "rideau" de cadres d'acier mobiles. Ils ont souhaité utiliser du plastique transparent et translucide coloré pour les garnir. Selon leur position, les éléments créent divers degrés d'intimité et plongent les contours de la ville dans le jaune, le rouge et le bleu - pour des perspectives inhabituelles. La nuit, le pavillon illuminé met une touche de couleur sur l'horizon habituellement noir du sud.

Un salotto all'aperto sul tetto di un magazzino degli anni venti è stata la richiesta di questo committente della costruzione, che fosse adatto sia per una cena intima sia per grandi eventi, isolato per un bagno di sole con contemporanea vista sulla città. Gli architetti della Johnsen Schmaling hanno proposto un gazebo sopra i tetti con una "tenda" fatta con cornici in acciaio spostabili. Per il riempimento sono stati previsti dei materiali plastici colorati trasparenti e traslucidi. A seconda della posizione gli elementi creano una quantità differente di area privata e colorano i contorni della città di giallo, rosso e blu - una vista inusuale. Di notte il gazebo illuminato pone un accento nella skyline a sud della città, che di norma resta nell'oscurità.

JOHNSTON MARKLEE | LOS ANGELES (CA), USA

Website	www.johnstonmarklee.com
Project	Sale House
Location	Venice (CA), USA
Year of Completion	2004
Building Materials	Wood frame structure with stucco finish
Color Specifications	Walls painted contrasting colors, including vivid pink, turquoise, orange-yellow, red and blue
Photo Credits	Eric Staudenmaier Photography, www.ericstaudenmaier.com

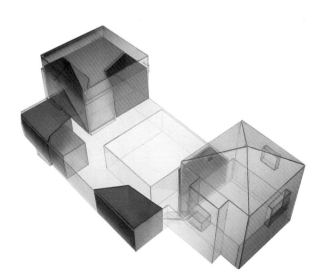

The cubic Sale House by Johnston Marklee—constructed in a typical residential settlement in California's Venice—is reminiscent of the Bauhaus style and therefore of its predecessor building, a bungalow from 1920. In the interior of the platonic body, the private areas sparkle in light pink, turquoise, and yellow-orange. The studio windows intentionally deviate from this approach in the primary colors of red, blue, and yellow. The white walls of the living spaces reflect these pulsating colors. The outer façade in neutral gray forms a stark contrast to the lively palette of colors. While the light and paint give the private rooms a dynamic feeling, the living area has a more transparent effect and refers more strongly to the outer world.

Das kubische Sale House von Johnston Marklee, errichtet in einer typischen Wohnsiedlung im kalifornischen Venice, erinnert an den Bauhaus Stil und somit an sein Vorgänger-Gebäude, einen Bungalow aus dem Jahr 1920. Im Inneren der platonischen Körper erstrahlen die privaten Räumlichkeiten in hellem Pink, Türkis und Gelb-Orange. Gewollt weichen hiervon die Studio-Fenster in den Grundfarben Rot, Blau und Gelb ab. Die weißen Wände der Wohnräume reflektieren diese pulsierenden Farben. Die Außenfassade bildet in neutralem Grau einen starken Kontrast zur lebendigen Farbpalette. Während Licht und Anstrich den Privatgemächern Dynamik verleihen, wirkt der Wohnbereich transparenter und nimmt stärker Bezug zur Außenwelt.

La Casa Sale, un diseño cúbico de Johnston Marklee, se levanta en un asentamiento residencial típico de la ciudad californiana de Venice. Recuerda al estilo bauhaus y, por consiguiente, a la construcción que le precede: un bungalow de 1920. En su interior, las estancias privadas deslumbran con su rosa claro, turquesa o amarillo anaranjado. Las ventanas del estudio difieren de forma intencionada de este tratamiento y se presentan en colores primarios: rojo, azul y amarillo. Las paredes blancas del salón reflejan estos colores tan vibrantes. La fachada exterior, en un gris neutral, contrasta con la paleta tan colorida. Mientras que la luz y los colores de las estancias privadas transmiten dinamismo, el efecto del salón es más transparente y está más conectado al mundo exterior.

La Sale House cubique de Johnston Marklee – construite dans un lotissement résidentiel typique de Venice, Californie – rappelle le style Bauhaus et donc le bâtiment précédent, un bungalow de 1920. A l'intérieur du solide de Platon, les zones privées étincellent en rose clair, turquoise et jaune-orangé. Les fenêtres du studio dévient intentionnellement de cette approche des couleurs primaires, rouge, bleu et jaune. Les murs blancs des espaces de vie reflètent ces couleurs vibrantes. La façade extérieure gris neutre forme un contraste parfait à cette palette de couleurs animées. Alors que la lumière et la peinture confèrent aux pièces privées une sensation de dynamisme, la zone séjour évoque davantage la transparence et se réfère plus fortement au monde extérieur.

La cubica Sale House di Johnston Marklee, costruita in un tipico complesso residenziale della californiana Venice, ricorda lo stile Bauhaus e quindi l'edificio suo predecessore, un bungalow del 1920. All'interno del corpo platonico si irradiano i locali privati con un rosa chiaro, turchese e giallo-arancione. Le finestre dello studio ne prendono intenzionalmente le distanze con i colori di base rosso, blu e giallo. Le pareti bianche dei locali riflettono questi colori pulsanti. La facciata esterna costituisce, con il suo grigio neutrale, un forte contrasto con la varietà di colori vivaci. Mentre la luce e la pittura donano della dinamicità agli ambienti privati, la zona soggiorno appare più trasparente e si riferisce più al mondo esterno.

KARIM RASHID | NEW YORK (NY), USA

Website	www.karimrashid.com
Project	Deutsche Bank Lounge
Project's website	www.db-artmag.com
Location	Cologne, Germany
Year of Completion	2006
Building Materials	Steel, dry mortarless construction, custom print film for walls, mirror elements, chrome metal sheets and LED backlit panels
Color Specifications	Colors: blue (as the DB logo), cyan, pink and white. Main gallery space: black and white. Side rooms: bicolor digital ornaments on the walls. Small meeting rooms: blue and lime. Bar area: cyan, blue and pink
Photo Credits	Lukas Roth, www.lukas-roth.de

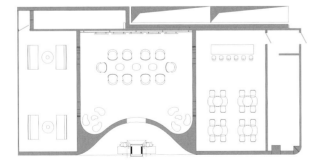

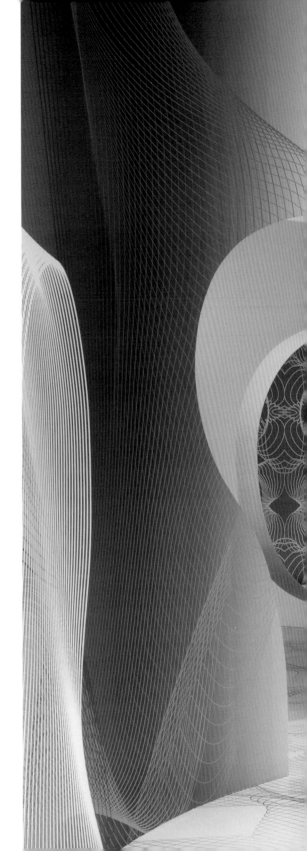

For the 40th Art Fair in Cologne, the Deutsche Bank presented itself with a VIP lounge as a discussion forum and with a selection of artworks. Visitors enter the lounge through a series of reflections and refractions of light, color, and patterns. Designer Karim Rashid decorated the space of the lounge with curvy walls and ceilings that "highlight the presence of artworks." Some of his design objects are in the side rooms; the areas with backlit floors offer a more intimate atmosphere. Fluorescent color marks the transition between the rooms. The wallpaper, also designed by the New Yorker, blurs the boundaries between architecture, design, and art.

Zur 40. Kunstmesse in Köln präsentierte sich die Deutsche Bank mit einer VIP Lounge als Diskussionsforum und mit einer Auswahl an Kunstwerken. Der Besucher betritt die Lounge durch eine Reihe von Reflexionen und Brechungen von Licht, Farbe und Mustern. Den Raum der Lounge gestaltet der Designer Karim Rashid mit kurvigen Wänden und Decken, welche „die Präsenz von Kunstwerken unterstreichen". In Seitenräumen finden sich einige seiner Designobjekte, die Bereiche mit hinterleuchtetem Fußboden bieten eine intimere Atmosphäre. Fluoreszierende Farbe markiert den Übergang zwischen den Räumen. Die Tapeten, auch von dem New Yorker entworfen, verwischen die Grenzen zwischen Architektur, Design und Kunst.

Con motivo de la 40ª Feria del Arte de Colonia, el Deutsche Bank se presentó con una sala VIP a modo de foro de diálogo y con una selección de obras de arte. El visitante accede a la sala atravesando una serie de reflejos y refracciones de luz, color y formas. El espacio del lounge, del diseñador Karim Rashid, tiene paredes y techos combados que "subrayan la presencia de las obras de arte". En las estancias adyacentes se encuentran algunos de sus diseños. Las zonas con pavimento luminoso ofrecen un ambiente más íntimo. Los colores fluorescentes marcan el paso entre los espacios. Los papeles pintados, también diseñados por el artista neoyorquino, diluyen las fronteras entre arquitectura, diseño y arte.

Pour la 40ème Foire d'Art de Cologne, la Deutsche Bank présentait un lounge VIP servant de forum de discussion et une sélection d'œuvres d'art. Les visiteurs entraient dans le lounge via une série de réflexions et de déflections de lumière, de couleur et de motifs. Le designer Karim Rashid a décoré l'espace du lounge avec des murs et des plafonds courbes qui « soulignent la présence des œuvres d'art ». Certains des objets qu'il a conçus sont dans les pièces latérales : les espaces avec des sols rétro-éclairés offrent une atmosphère plus intime. La couleur fluorescente indique la transition entre les pièces. Le papier peint, également conçu par le newyorkais, estompe les frontières entre architecture, design et art.

In occasione della 40. fiera dell'arte a Colonia la Deutsche Bank si è presentata con una VIP lounge per un forum di discussione e con una selezione di opere d'arte. Il visitatore accede alla lounge tramite una serie di riflessi e rifrazioni di luce, colore e disegni. Il designer Karim Rashid ha strutturato lo spazio della lounge con pareti e soffitti ricurvi che "sottolineano la presenza di opere d'arte". Nelle sale laterali si trovano alcuni dei suoi oggetti di design, le zone con il pavimento retroilluminato offrono una atmosfera più intima. Il colore fluorescente marca il passaggio tra le stanze. Le carte da parati, anch'esse progettate dal newyorchese, sfumano i confini tra architettura, design e arte.

KARIM RASHID | NEW YORK (NY), USA

Website	www.karimrashid.com
Project	Karim Rashid's Loft
Location	New York (NY), USA
Year of Completion	2000
Building Materials	Wall coverings and wall paper designed by Karim Rashid, poured rubber epoxy floors, curvet glass, vidrepur glass tiles, carpet field
Color Specifications	Yellow glass wall between bathroom and living space; bathroom: fluorescent lime, black high-gloss morphscape pattern laminate floor; living space: fluorescent orange; rear area: pink carpet field; kitchen: morphscape white plastic laminate cupboards
Photo Credits	Jean Francois Jaussaud, France

Karim Rashid is not afraid of dynamic colors and organic forms—he also proves this in his own New York Loft: glossy white epoxy flooring, a touch of fluorescent orange, a pink rug in the front area, and light green in the bathroom. The designer has inherited a certain quality from his father: The film architect loves moving around the furniture every month. And so it is unlikely that the loft still looks like the original plan because the designer describes it as a gallery and brings home new prototypes on a regular basis. Karim Rashid loves it when he sees that people live in a contemporary way and free themselves from nostalgia and antiquated traditions.

Karim Rashid hat keine Angst vor dynamischen Farben und organischen Formen - das beweist er auch in seinem eigenen New Yorker Loft: glänzender, weißer Epoxydharzboden, ein Hauch fluoreszierendes Orange, im vorderen Bereich ein rosa Teppich, Hellgrün im Bad. Eine Eigenschaft hat der Designer von seinem Vater geerbt. Der Filmarchitekt liebte monatliches Möbelrücken. Und so ist es unwahrscheinlich, dass das Loft noch wie geplant aussieht, zumal der Designer es selbst als Galerie beschreibt, und regelmäßig neue Prototypen mit nach Hause bringt. Karim Rashid liebt es, wenn er sieht, dass Menschen in einer zeitgemäßen Art leben und sich von Nostalgie und antiquierten Traditionen befreien.

Karim Rashid no se amedrenta ante los colores dinámicos y las formas orgánicas, algo que queda patente en su propio loft neoyorquino. Suelos de Epoxy en blanco brillante, un toque en naranja fluorescente, en la entrada una alfombra rosa y el baño en verde claro. El artista heredó una cualidad de su padre: al diseñador cinematográfico le encanta mover los muebles de sitio todos los meses, por lo que es poco probable que el loft sea como se diseñó en un principio. El diseñador lo define como una "galería" a la que lleva con regularidad nuevos prototipos. A Karim Rashid le encanta que la gente viva de forma actual y liberada de la nostalgia y las tradiciones anticuadas.

Karim Rashid n'a pas peur des couleurs dynamiques et des formes organiques – il le prouve aussi dans son propre loft newyorkais : un sol en époxy blanc brillant, une touche d'orange fluorescent, un tapis rose dans la zone avant et une lumière verte dans la salle de bain. Le designer a hérité d'une qualité de son père : l'architecte de cinéma aime déplacer ses meubles tous les mois. Et il est donc peu probable que le loft garde l'apparence du plan originel, car le designer le décrit comme une galerie et ramène régulièrement de nouveaux prototypes à la maison. Karim Rashid adore voir les gens vivre de manière contemporaine en se libérant de la nostalgie et des traditions désuètes.

Karim Rashid non ha paura di colori dinamici e di forme organiche – questo lo dimostra anche nel suo loft di New York: un pavimento in resina lucido e bianco, un velo di arancione fluorescente, nell'area antistante un tappeto rosa, verde chiaro in bagno. Il designer ha ereditato una caratteristica da suo padre. L'architetto di film amava spostare i mobili ogni mese. E così è improbabile che il loft abbia ancora l'aspetto di come è stato progettato, soprattutto perchè il designer stesso lo descrive come una galleria e si porta costantemente nuovi prototipi in casa. A Karim Rashid piace vedere le persone vivere in un modo conforme ai tempi e liberarsi dalla nostalgia e da tradizioni antiquate.

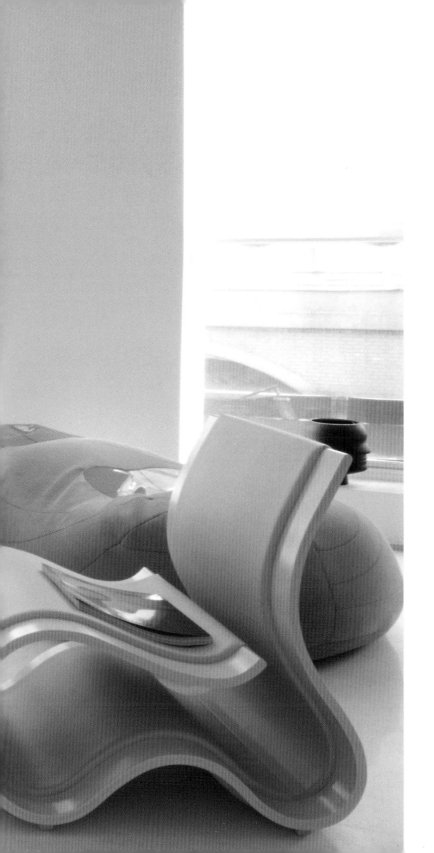

KARIM RASHID | NEW YORK (NY), USA

Website	www.karimrashid.com
Project	Semiramis Hotel
Location	Athens, Greece
Year of Completion	2004
Building Materials	Steel, dry mortarless construction, terrazzo slabs, glass tiles, teak wood, epoxy floors, carpet, glass, Rashid-designed patterned wall coverings, laminate surfaces, other contemporary finishes
Color Specifications	Exterior: covered in traditional small, high-gloss white ceramic tiles, canvas predominantly white, pink, lime green, orange, and yellow.
	Interior: glowing colored glass cube leading into lobby, colorful carpeting inlaid into white glossy epoxy floors, restaurant encased in orange glass, different color concepts for each room
Photo Credits	Vagelis Paterakis (p 193, excl. top left image), Jean Francois Jaussaud, France

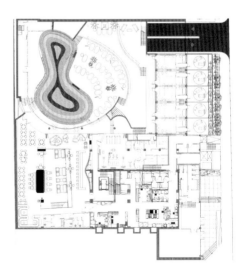

A quote from Karim Rashid is characteristic for the Semiramis Hotel: "Hotels today make you feel like you're living in the previous century. That's the last thing I wanted to do." The New Yorker describes the hotel as a "mélange of technology, art, and a sensibility of infosthetics." The guests do not find their room using a number; instead, a symbol shows the way to the colorful accommodations. From frosted-glass bathrooms, in part with rounded wall corners, colorful carpet on glossy epoxy floors, to the furniture and the little shampoo bottles—everything comes from one source. The hotel is oriented upon the international focus that Athens has experienced since the 2004 Olympic Games.

Bezeichnend für das Semiramis Hotel ist ein Zitat von Karim Rashid: „Hotels heute geben einem das Gefühl, in einem vergangenen Jahrhundert zu wohnen. Das ist das Letzte, was ich wollte." Der New Yorker beschreibt das Hotel als eine „Mélange aus Technologie, Kunst und Sensibilität für Infostetics". Die Gäste finden ihren Raum nicht anhand einer Nummer, sondern ein Symbol zeigt den Weg zur farbenfrohen Unterkunft. Von „glasierten" Badezimmern, zum Teil abgerundeten Wandecken, farbigen Teppichen auf glänzendem Epoxydharzböden über das Mobilar bis hin zum Shampoo-Fläschchen – alles stammt aus einer Hand. Das Hotel richtet sich an die internationale Aufmerksamkeit, die Athen seit den Olympischen Spielen 2004 erfährt.

Una cita de Karim Rashid define el Hotel Semiramis: "En los hoteles de hoy tienes la impresión de estar viviendo en el siglo pasado. Eso es lo último que quiero hacer". El neoyorquino define este hotel como un "cóctel de tecnología, arte y sensibilidad por la infoestética". Los huéspedes encuentran su habitación no por el número, sino por un símbolo que les guía hasta su colorido alojamiento. Desde el baño de cristal esmerilado, paredes parcialmente encorvadas, alfombras de colores y suelos de deslumbrante Epoxy, hasta el mobiliario y los champús: todo es obra de la misma persona. El hotel va dirigido a un público internacional del que goza Atenas desde los Juegos Olímpicos de 2004.

Une citation de Karim Rashid caractérise parfaitement l'Hôtel Semiramis : « Les hôtels d'aujourd'hui vous donnent l'impression de vivre au siècle dernier. C'est la dernière chose que je voulais faire. » Le newyorkais décrit l'hôtel comme un « mélange de technologie, d'art et de sensibilité de l'infosthétique. » Les clients ne trouvent pas leur chambre grâce à des numéros, mais un symbole montre le chemin vers les chambres colorées. Des salles de bains givrées, comportant des murs courbes et des tapis colorés sur des sols en époxy brillant, aux meubles et aux petites bouteilles de shampooing, tout provient de la même source. L'hôtel vise l'attention internationale dont bénéficie Athènes depuis les Jeux Olympiques de 2004.

Significativo per il Semiramis Hotel è una citazione di Karim Rashid: "Gli alberghi oggigiorno danno l'impressione di abitare in un secolo passato. Questa è l'ultima cosa che volevo al mondo." Il newyorchese descrive l'albergo come una "miscela di tecnologia, arte e sensibilità per infostetics". Gli ospiti non trovano le loro stanze grazie a dei numeri, ma un simbolo mostra la strada verso l'alloggio raggiante di colori: sale da bagno "smaltate a vetro", spigoli parzialmente arrotondati, un tappeto colorato su pavimenti in resina fino alla mobilia o alla bottiglietta per lo shampoo – tutto è stato fatto da una sola manifattura. L'albergo punta verso il fuoco internazionale che Atene vive dai Giochi Olimpici del 2004.

KEN ARCHITEKTEN BSA | BADEN, ZURICH, SWITZERLAND

Website	www.ken-architekten.ch
Project	Wonderland Kindergarten
Location	Dietikon, Switzerland
Year of Completion	2005
Building Materials	Massive construction, reinforced concrete, interior insulation, mineral wool, cladding, drywall, cork linoleum, wood/metal windows, fitted furniture of derived-timber-product boards, artificial turf
Color Specifications	Vibrant color focused on window frames and furniture
Photo Credits	Hannes Henz, Zürich

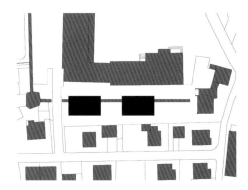

A 246 feet long battlement wall becomes the structure-determining element of Wunderland (Wonderland), two nursery schools in the Swiss city of Dietikon. In the interior of the two hall-like buildings—which optically appear to be on tracks as they are set on a washed-concrete terrace—the core of the infrastructure with large, dark-red sliding doors sets accents and the floor space is kept in a brilliant orange. The window frames project far into the room. The play of the window niches with varying depths at the height of the children's tables is supported by the bright series of colors. The walls have been clad with perforated drywall boards in a warm shade of gray. Together with the moon-like lamps, this awakens associations with a starry sky.

Eine 75 m lange Festungsmauer wird zum strukturbestimmenden Element von „Wunderland", zweier Kindergärten im schweizerischen Dietikon. Im Inneren der beiden hallenartigen Bauten – die auf eine Waschbetonstufe aufgelegt, optisch wie auf Schienen laufen – setzt der Infrastrukturkern mit großen, dunkelroten Schiebetüren Akzente, die Nutzflächen sind leuchtend orange gehalten. Fensterrahmen ragen weit in den Raum hinein. Das Spiel der unterschiedlich tiefen Fensternischen auf Kindertisch-Höhe wird unterstützt durch die bunte Farbreihe. Die Wände sind mit gelochten Gipskartonplatten in einem warmen Grauton verkleidet, gemeinsam mit mondartigen Leuchten wird die Assoziation mit einem Sternenhimmel geweckt.

Un muro de cercado de 75 m de largo se convierte en elemento estructural del "Mundo Encantado", dos guarderías de la ciudad suiza de Dietikon. Estas dos construcciones en forma de nave reposan en estribos de hormigón de árido visto, dando la sensación óptica de estar sobre raíles. Su interior está marcado estructuralmente por grandes puertas correderas en rojo, mientras que la superficie de uso es naranja. Los marcos de las ventanas sobresalen por el interior. La profundidad dispar de los vanos de las ventanas a la altura de las mesas es un juego que se sirve de la secuencia en diferentes colores. Las paredes están recubiertas con placas agujereadas de escayola en un gris cálido que, junto a las luminarias en forma de Luna, podrían asemejarse al firmamento.

Un mur d'enceinte de 75 m de long est l'élément de structure déterminant de Wunderland (Pays des Merveilles), deux écoles maternelles dans la ville suisse de Dietikon. A l'intérieur des deux bâtiments ressemblant à des halls – qui à l'œil nu paraissent être sur des rails parce que fixés sur une terrasse en béton lavé – le noyau des infrastructures, avec ses large portes coulissantes rouge foncé, donne le ton, alors que l'espace au sol est d'un orange brillant. Les chassis de fenêtre se projettent loin dans la pièce. Le jeu de profondeur des embrasures, à la hauteur des tables d'enfants, est renforcé par un ensemble de couleurs vives. Les murs sont revêtus de plaques de cloison sèche d'une nuance chaude de gris. Associés aux lampes en forme de lune, ils évoquent un ciel étoilé.

Il muro della fortezza lungo 75 m diventa l'elemento del "paese delle meraviglie" che definisce la struttura di due asili infantili nel Dietikon svizzero. All'interno degli edifici a forma di capannone – che, essendo stati costruiti su un gradino di calcestruzzo lavato, dal punto di vista ottico sembrano correre su dei binari – il cuore dell'infrastruttura pone degli accenti con delle grandi porte scorrevoli rosso-scure; le superfici utili vengono tenute in un arancione lucido. Delle cornici delle finestre entrano ampiamente nella stanza. Il gioco delle nicchie per le finestre con delle profondità variabili e ad altezza dei tavoli dei bambini viene supportato tramite una serie di vari colori. Le pareti sono rivestite con pannelli di cartongesso forato in un tono caldo di grigio; insieme a dei lumi a forma di luna viene risvegliata l'idea di un cielo stellato.

DENIS KOSUTIC | VIENNA, AUSTRIA

Website	www.deniskosutic.com
Project	Penthouse A
Location	Vienna, Austria
Year of Completion	2007
Building Materials	Floor: Pandomo; ceilings: color dispersion; wall coverings: plaited leather, Dedar, ostrich-embossed leather, drapery; built-in furniture: matt-painted MDF, glass mosaic tiles
Color Specifications	Color concept: colors and non-colors; dark violet, carmine and crimson
Photo Credits	Rupert Steiner, Vienna

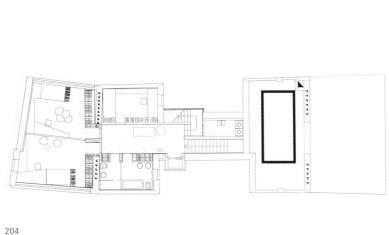

Denis Kosutic has created a Viennese homage to the Florentine Renaissance in the realization of a penthouse on three levels. In the entrance and passage areas, dramatic color compositions produce a subdued atmosphere together with mysterious, theatrical moods. The hall and adjacent areas are characterized by intensive colors: dark violet, crimson, and blood-red alternate with animal prints and Asiatic battle scenes on the wall elements. Black and white, as "non-colors" set exciting counterpoints in the private rooms and play with textures: Seating furniture and tables are covered with reptile leather, the wall are lacquered or covered with woven leather.

Denis Kosutic erschafft mit der Realisierung eines Penthouses auf drei Ebenen eine Wiener Hommage an die florentinische Renaissance. In den Eingangs- und Durchgangsflächen erzeugen dramatische Farbkompositionen eine gedämpfte Atmosphäre und zugleich geheimnisvolle, theatralische Stimmungen. Die Halle und die Erschließungsflächen sind von intensiven Farben geprägt: Dunkelviolett, Karminrot und Blutrot wechseln sich mit Tierdrucken und asiatischen Kampfszenen auf Wandelementen ab. Schwarz und Weiß, als „Nichtfarben" setzen spannende Kontrapunkte in den Privaträumen und spielen mit Texturen: Sitzmöbel und Tische sind mit Reptilienleder überzogen, Wände lackiert oder mit geflochtenem Leder bespannt.

Denis Kosutic ha realizado un homenaje vienés al renacimiento florentino mediante un ático de tres plantas. En las paredes del recibidor y el pasillo, unas composiciones cromáticas cargadas de dramatismo generan una atmósfera contenida al tiempo que misteriosa y teatral. En el vestíbulo y el paso a la estancia, los colores son intensos: violeta oscuro, rojo carmín y rojo sangre se combinan con huellas animales, escenas de batallas asiáticas y elementos en las paredes. Blanco y negro, considerados "incoloros", dan lugar a interesantes contrastes en las estancias privadas y juegan con las texturas de sillas y mesas, tapizadas con pieles de reptiles, y con las de las paredes, pintadas o revestidas con entramados de piel.

Denis Kosutic a créé un hommage viennois à la Renaissance florentine en réalisant un appartement-terrasse (penthouse) sur trois niveaux. Dans les zones d'entrée et de passage, de spectaculaires compositions de couleurs produisent une atmosphère discrète associée à des ambiances mystérieuses, théâtrales. Le hall et les zones adjacentes sont caractérisés par des couleurs intenses : violet foncé, pourpre et rouge sang alternent avec imprimés animaux et scènes de batailles asiatiques sur les éléments muraux. Le noir et le blanc, en tant qu'ensemble « non-couleur », offrent un contrepoint stimulant dans les pièces privées et jouent avec les textures : les meubles d'assise et les tables sont couverts de cuir de reptile, les murs sont laqués et couverts de cuir tramé.

Denis Kosutic ha creato un Wiener Hommage (omaggio viennese) al rinascimento fiorentino con la realizzazione di una Penthouse su tre livelli. Nelle aree di entrata e di passaggio delle composizioni drammatiche di colori creano un'atmosfera smorzata e al tempo stesso delle suggestioni misteriose e teatrali. Il salone e le aree di apertura sono segnati da colori intensivi: viola scuro, rosso carminio e rosso sangue si alternano con stampe di animali e scene di caccia asiatiche raffigurati su elementi di pareti. Nero e bianco, in qualità di "non-colori" appongono degli avvincenti contrappunti nelle camere private e giocano con i tessuti: mobili per sedersi e tavoli sono rivestiti con pelle di rettili, le pareti sono laccate o sono ricoperte con pelle intrecciata.

KRESING ARCHITEKTEN | MÜNSTER, GERMANY

Website	www.kresing.de
Project	Brillux—Administration Building and Customer Center
Location	Münster, Germany
Year of Completion	2004
Building Materials	Reinforced-concrete skeleton construction, wood-composite building panels, glass, light strip of polycarbonate, ceilings: acoustic plaster, floor: flashed granite, carpets, cast stone 1.3 x 1.3 feet, walls: reinforced concrete, non-supportive walls in dry construction
Color Specifications	More than color. The entire world of colorfulness and creativity is presented and supported by a black band. Just like the line giving a foundation to a painting, black and white serve as a tableau for development and vision.
Photo Credits	Christian Richters, Münster

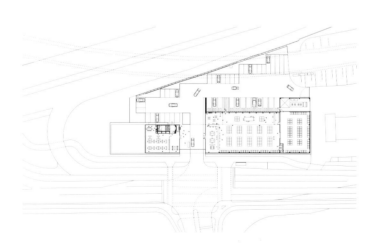

The Brillux Building optically symbolizes both the colorfulness of the program and the clarity in the company philosophy. Kresing Architekten rely on black and white as a platform. As the backdrop for color, black and white create a maximum of trust, solidity, and elegance. Black-and-white surfaces—supported by the transparency of glass—offer space for vivid, multicolored possibilities, for creativity. The customer center, designed as a white box, is connected with the five-story tower in the front through a black horizontal and vertically running band. Polychromatism and variety are concentrated and set in relationship to each other through clear form and use of lines. Within this context, the colors are presented by black and white.

Das Brillux-Gebäude symbolisiert optisch die Farbigkeit des Angebots und gleichzeitig die Klarheit in der Unternehmensphilosophie. Kresing Architekten setzen auf Schwarz und Weiß als Plattform, als Träger für Farbe. Schwarz und Weiß schaffen ein Maximum an Vertrauen, Solidität und Eleganz. Schwarz-weiße Flächen – unterstützt von Transparenz aus Glas – bieten den Raum für leuchtende, vielfarbige Möglichkeiten, für Kreativität. Das Kundencenter, als weiße Box gestaltet, ist mit dem vorgelagerten, fünfgeschossigen Turm durch ein schwarzes horizontal und vertikal verlaufendes Band verbunden. Vielfarbigkeit und Vielfältigkeit werden gebündelt und zueinander in Beziehung gesetzt durch klare Formen und Linienführung. Dabei präsentieren Schwarz und Weiß Farbe.

El edificio Brillux simboliza de forma visual el colorido de la oferta y, al tiempo, la claridad de la filosofía de la empresa. Los arquitectos de Kresing se decidieron por una base en blanco y negro como paleta para los colores. Blanco y negro son la expresión máxima de la confianza, la solidez y la elegancia. Las superficies en blanco y negro – favorecidas por la transparencia del cristal – le dan al espacio posibilidades luminosas y coloristas, le dan creatividad. El centro de atención al cliente, concebido como un cubo blanco, está unido a la torre de cinco alturas por una plataforma negra que va en dirección vertical y horizontal. La riqueza cromática y la variedad se asocian e interactúan mediante formas y trazados claros, para lo cual el blanco y el negro son perfectos.

L'immeuble Brillux symbolise visuellement à la fois la couleur du programme et la clarté de la philosophie de l'entreprise. Kresing Architekten se sert du blanc et du noir comme plateforme. Toile de fond pour la couleur, le noir et le blanc créent un maximum de confiance, de solidité et d'élégance. Les surfaces en noir et blanc – renforcées par la transparence du verre – offrent un espace pour des possibilités intenses et multicolores, pour la créativité. Le centre client, conçu comme une boîte blanche, est connecté à l'avant avec la tour de cinq étages à travers une bande noire horizontale et verticale. Le polychromatisme et la variété sont concentrés et définis en relation mutuelle via des formes et des lignes claires. Dans ce contexte, les couleurs sont présentées par le noir et le blanc.

L'edificio Brillux simboleggia dal punto di vista ottico la varietà dei colori dell'offerta e al contempo la chiarezza nella filosofia dell'azienda. Gli architetti della Kresing hanno puntato sul bianco e nero per la piattaforma, come portatore di colori. Il nero e il bianco creano una fiducia, una solidarietà e un'eleganza estrema. Delle superfici nero-bianche – supportate dalla trasparenza di vetro – offrono lo spazio per delle occasioni luminose colorate e per della creatività. Il centro assistenza per i clienti, realizzato in forma di una scatola bianca, è collegato con la torre preposta di cinque piani attraverso un nastro nero che corre orizzontalmente e verticalmente. La policromia e la molteplicità vengono legate insieme e portate in relazione l'una con l'altra attraverso delle forme e un tratteggio chiari. Così il nero e il bianco presentano il colore.

KRESING ARCHITEKTEN | MÜNSTER, GERMANY

Website	www.kresing.de
Project	Freiherr-vom-Stein-Gymnasium
Location	Münster, Germany
Year of Completion	2006
Building Materials	Thermal-insulation composite system with paint coating and green sunscreens
Photo Credits	Christian Richters, Münster

The **Kresing Architekten** from Münster understand school as a process of cultural growth and development instead of a secluded area for education. This concept is also reflected in the design idea: An educational garden that stimulates the senses, promotes creativity, and supports concentration. The school and its grounds offer a variety of fields for different uses. The green color moves in "waves" through the parts of the building and symbolizes the—almost literally—flowing transition between the green interior areas and the external area that is just as green. For the architects, green means growth and development, concentration and consciousness, inspiration and life.

Schule ist für die Kresing Architekten aus Münster nicht ein abgegrenzter Bereich für Bildung, sondern wird verstanden als ein Prozess von kulturellem Wachsen und Werden. Dies spiegelt sich in der Entwurfsidee wider: ein Bildungsgarten, der die Sinne anregt, die Kreativität fördert, die Konzentration unterstützt. Die Schule und ihr Gelände bieten unterschiedliche Felder für verschiedene Nutzungen. Die grüne Farbe bewegt sich in „Wellen" durch die Gebäudeteile und symbolisiert den – somit fast wörtlich – fließenden Übergang zwischen dem grünen Innen- und ebenso grünen Außenbereich. Grün bedeutet für die Architekten Wachstum und Entwicklung, Konzentration und Besinnung, Inspiration und Leben.

Para los arquitectos Kresing de la ciudad alemana de Münster, la escuela no es un espacio delimitado destinado a la formación, sino que es entendido como un proceso de crecimiento cultural, lo que se refleja en el diseño: un jardín de aprendizaje que agudiza los sentidos, fomenta la creatividad y favorece la concentración. El colegio y sus instalaciones ofrecen diferentes espacios para usos diversos. El verde se mueve a modo de "ondas" a lo largo de las diferentes partes del edificio y simboliza - casi de forma literal - la transición fluida entre el interior en verde y el exterior del mismo color. Para los arquitectos, el verde representa crecimiento y desarrollo, concentración y reflexión, inspiración y vida.

Les architectes de Kresing Architekten, à Münster, voient l'école comme un processus de croissance et de développement culturels plutôt que comme un espace isolé pour l'éducation. Ce concept se reflète également dans l'idée de design : un jardin éducatif qui stimule les sens, encourage la créativité et aide à la concentration. L'école et ses terrains offrent des lieux variés pour différents usages. La couleur verte se déplace en « vagues » à travers les diverses parties du bâtiment et symbolise - quasiment littéralement - une transition fluide entre les zones vertes intérieures et l'espace extérieur, tout aussi vert. Pour les architectes, le vert signifie la croissance et le développement, la concentration et la conscience, l'inspiration et la vie.

Per gli architetti della Kresing di Münster la scuola non è un settore limitato alla formazione, ma viene inteso come un processo di crescita e un divenire culturali. Questo s rispecchia nell'idea del progetto: un giardino della formazione che stimola i sensi, che incentiva la creatività e supporta la concentrazione. La scuola e la sua area offrono differenti campi per diversi utilizzi. Il verde si snoda in „onde" attraverso le parti dell'edificio e simboleggia il - così quasi in senso letterale - passaggio fluente tra l'area interna verde e l'area esterna altrettanto verde. Il verde significa per gli architetti crescita e sviluppo, concentrazione e meditazione, ispirazione e vita.

THE LAWRENCE GROUP ARCHITECTS | NEW YORK (NY), USA

Website	www.thelawrencegroup.com/ny
Project	Momentum-St. Louis
Location	St. Louis (MO), USA
Year of Completion	2006
Building Materials	Painted drywall on metal studs, polished and stained concrete floors, lacquered MDF panels, acrylic resin panels, exposed ceilings and ductwork.
Color Specifications	Custom colored textured red wall paint—'Momentum Red', custom colored integral concrete floor colors, perforated stainless steel
Photo Credits	Frank Oudeman, New York; Alise O'Brien, St. Louis

Flowing, vivid, symbiotic—this is how viewers experience the interior when they enter the business premises of the Momentum agency in St Louis. The fundamental idea by the planners of the Lawrence Group was to depict the progressive, innovative Momentum brand through a sensual-vivid spatial experience. The interior is designed to stimulate creativity and plays with spatial, visual, and material interactions. The supporting element in the color scheme is the Momentum red in the form of an amorphous band. It shows the way to the reception desk, conference rooms, and work areas. Walls of transparent materials, digital projections, and oversized graphics complete the "Red Motif."

Fließend, eindringend, symbiotisch – so empfinden Betrachter das Interieur, wenn sie die Geschäftsräume der Agentur Momentum in St Louis betreten. Der Grundgedanke der Planer von Lawrence Group: die progressive, innovative Marke Momentum durch ein sinnlich-eindringliches Raum-Erlebnis darstellen. Das Interieur ist designt, um die Kreativität anzuregen, spielt mit räumlichen, visuellen und materiellen Wechselwirkungen. Das tragende Element in der Farbgestaltung ist das Momentum-Rot in Form eines amorphen Bandes. Es weist den Weg zu Rezeption, Konferenzräumen und Arbeitsbereichen. Wände aus transparenten Materialien, digitale Projektionen und überdimensionale Grafiken komplettieren die „Rote Botschaft".

Fluido, penetrante y simbiótico – De esta forma perciben el interior los que visitan las oficinas de la agencia Momentum de St. Louis (EE. UU.). La idea fundamental de los planificadores de Lawrence Group fue plasmar el carácter avanzado e innovador de la marca Momentum a través de una penetrante experiencia sensorial en sus instalaciones. El interior ha sido diseñado para estimular la creatividad y juega con la interacción espacial, visual y material. El peso en la escala cromática lo lleva el rojo Momentum en forma de banda sin forma definida que muestra el camino a la recepción, las salas de reunión y los despachos. Paredes de material transparente, proyecciones digitales y grafismos de gran tamaño completan el „lema rojo".

Fluctuant, intense, symbiotique – c'est ce qu'éprouvent les visiteurs à l'intérieur des locaux commerciaux de l'agence Momentum à St Louis. L'idée fondamentale des concepteurs du Lawrence Group était de dépeindre la marque Momentum, synonyme de progrès et d'innovation, à travers une expérience spaciale et sensuelle intense. L'intérieur est conçu pour stimuler la créativité et joue avec les interactions spaciales, visuelles et matérielles. L'élément de base de l'agencement des couleurs est le rouge Momentum, revêtant ici la forme d'une bande amorphe. Elle indique le chemin vers la réception, les salles de conférence et les espaces de travail. Des murs en matériaux transparents, des projections numériques et des graphismes démesurés complètent le « Motif rouge ».

Fluente, vivace, simbolico – così gli spettatori vivono l'interno, quando accedono ai locali commerciali della Momentum agency a St Louis. L'idea di base dei progettisti della Lawrence Group è stata quella di rappresentare il marchio progressista e innovativo della Momentum tramite un'esperienza dello spazio sensuale-vivace. L'interno è progettato per stimolare la creatività e gioca con interazioni spaziali, visuali e materiali. L'elemento supportante nella rappresentazione dei colori è il rosso Momentum in forma di un nastro amorfo. Esso mostra la strada per la reception, le sale conferenza e le aree di lavoro. Delle pareti di materiali trasparenti, delle proiezioni digitali e delle grafiche sovradimensionate completano il "motivo rosso".

LÖHMANN'S ARCHITECTURE · URBAN
+ INDUSTRIAL DESIGN | AMSTERDAM, NETHERLANDS

Website	www.loehmann.nl
Project	Heerema Marine Contractor
Location	Leiden, Netherlands
Year of Completion	2006
Building Materials	Space-defining surfaces: light materials that have a silvery shine such as aluminum, high-grade steel, glass concrete. Special function zones: matte, tactile materials such as 1-inch thick woven wool, wood, leather and rubber. Reception: polyester concrete. Walls, built-in closets, and ceilings in the conference area: anodized aluminum. Conference tables: highly polished, lacquered table tops in light gray; supporting frame of high-grade steel
Color Specifications	Floors in general: concrete with blue, green, and black color pigments. Special function zones: bright colors like red wool and leather for the waiting island; bright orange for the company name on the glass wall of the conference area; red, orange, and yellow chair covers
Photo Credits	Jannes Linders, Rotterdam

A more subtle but still powerful use of color is inside the office building. Together with the aluminum ceiling, concrete that has been stained green-blue is the backbone of the building and marks the areas that serve informal communication. Bright colors are employed in an accentuated way by Löhmann's Architecture in rooms with special functions. For example, they gave the fitness room a green rubber floor—with the same material for the counter—and the entrance hall is furnished with deep-red leather armchairs. The conference center assumes the most important representation function: The large letters of the company name decorate the dividing walls in the color of the logo: orange in color-coordination with the furnishings.

Ein zurückhaltender, aber trotzdem kraftvoller Farbeinsatz findet sich in dem Bürogebäude. Grün-blau gefärbter Beton bildet zusammen mit der Aluminiumdecke das Rückrat des Gebäudes und markiert die Flächen, die zur informellen Kommunikation dienen. Kräftige Farben setzen Löhmann's Architecture in Räumen mit besonderen Funktionen akzentuiert ein. So versehen sie den Fitnessraum mit grünem Gummi-Fußboden – im gleichen Material die Theke – und die Eingangshalle ist mit tiefroten Ledersesseln möbliert. Das Konferenzzentrum übernimmt die wichtigste Repräsentationsfunktion: Die großen Buchstaben des Firmennamens schmücken die Trennwände in der Farbe des Logos: Orange, in Farb-Abstimmung mit der Möblierung.

En este edificio de oficinas encontramos un uso de colores mesurado, pero a la vez enérgico. El hormigón en azul y verde, junto a los techos de aluminio, conforman la columna vertebral del edificio y marcan los espacios destinados a la comunicación informal. Los colores más fuertes acentúan la arquitectura de Löhmann en los espacios con funciones específicas. Por ejemplo, el gimnasio dispone de un piso de goma verde – el mostrador es del mismo material –; el vestíbulo se ha amueblado con sillones de cuero en un rojo intenso. La sala de conferencias desempeña la principal función representativa: las letras de gran tamaño que componen el nombre de la empresa decoran el tabique divisorio con los colores del logotipo: naranja en consonancia con los colores del mobiliario.

L'utilisation des couleurs est plus subtile mais toujours puissante à l'intérieur de l'immeuble de bureaux. Avec le plafond en aluminium, le béton coloré en vert-bleu sert d'ossature centrale au bâtiment et indique les zones qui permettent la communication informelle. Les couleurs vives sont utilisées de manière appuyée par Löhmann's Architecture dans les pièces ayant des fonctions spéciales. Par exemple, ils ont doté la salle de fitness d'un sol en caoutchouc vert – avec le même matériau pour le comptoir – et le hall d'entrée est meublé de fauteuils en cuir rouge profond. Le centre de conférence joue la fonction représentative la plus importante : les larges lettres du nom de l'entreprise décorent les murs de séparations dans la couleur du logo, orange, en coordination de couleur avec les meubles.

Nell'edificio adibito agli uffici si trova un utilizzo di colore più discreto, ma comunque energico. Del cemento colorato verde-blu costituisce insieme al soffitto in alluminio lo schienale per l'edificio e segna le aree che servono a una comunicazione informale. La Löhmann's Architecture ha utilizzato in modo accentuato dei colori forti nelle stanze con funzioni particolari. Così la zona fitness è stata attrezzata con un pavimento in gomma verde – il bancone è dello stesso materiale – e la sala d'ingresso è stata arredata con sedie in pelle rosso forte. Il centro conferenza è stato incaricato della funzione rappresentativa più importante: le grandi lettere del nome della ditta decorano le pareti divisorie nel colore del logo: arancione, in armonia con i colori della mobilia.

MAGMA ARCHITECTURE | BERLIN, GERMANY

Website	www.magmaarchitecture.com
Project	head in	im kopf
Location	Berlinische Galerie, State Museum of Modern Art, Photography and Architecture, Berlin, Germany
Year of Completion	2007
Building Materials	Textiles, aluminum, stretch color (polyamide, elastan)
Color Specifications	Orange fabric
Photo Credits	Johanna Diehl, Berlin; Dominik Jörg, Berlin

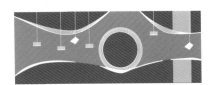

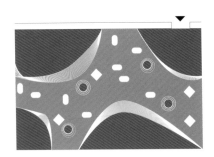

The focus of the exhibition head in | im kopf is the amorphous spatial sculpture, designed for the 492 sq. ft. special showroom in the Berlinische Galerie. When visitors get immersed in the orange-colored exhibition architecture, this means actively learning about the inner life of the sculpture—a new, surprising experience. The color in the exhibition appears to be less of an enveloping surface and more like an orange mass through which the visitor moves as an observer. magma architecture achieved this effect partially through amorphous forms that allow the boundaries of the space to disappear, as well as through reflections of the color, people, models, and drawings that give it an orange glow.

Mittelpunkt der Ausstellung head in | im kopf ist die amorphe Raumskulptur, entworfen für den 150 m² großen Sonderausstellungsraum in der Berlinischen Galerie. In die orangefarbene Ausstellungsarchitektur einzutauchen, bedeutet für Besucher, sich das Innenleben der Skulptur aktiv anzueignen. Eine neue, überraschende Erfahrung. Farbe erscheint in der Ausstellung weniger als umhüllende Fläche, sondern wie eine orangene Masse, durch die man sich als Betrachter bewegt. magma architecture erreichen diese Wirkung teilweise durch amorphe Formen, die die Grenzen des Raumes verschwinden lassen, aber auch durch Reflexionen der Farbe, die Personen, Modellen und Zeichnungen einen orangenen Schein verleihen.

El foco de atención de la exposición head in | im kopf es una escultura espacial informe diseñada para la sala de exposiciones extraordinarias de 150 m² de la Berlinische Galerie. Sumergirse en la arquitectura de esta pieza de color naranja significa para el visitante adentrarse de forma activa en la vida interior de la escultura. Una experiencia nueva y sorprendente. El color en esta exposición no es tanto una superficie envolvente como una masa naranja por la que el observador puede moverse. magma architecture ha conseguido este efecto en parte gracias a las líneas informes que se pierden en los límites del espacio, pero también mediante reflejos cromáticos que otorgan a personas, maquetas y dibujos una coloración anaranjada.

Le clou de l'exposition head in | im kopf est la sculpture spatiale amorphe conçue pour la salle d'exposition spéciale de 150 m² de Berlinische Galerie. Quand les visiteurs s'immergent dans l'architecture orange de l'exposition, ils peuvent apprendre beaucoup, de manière active, sur la vie intérieure de la sculpture – une expérience nouvelle, surprenante. La couleur de l'exposition apparaît moins comme une surface enveloppante que comme une masse orange à travers laquelle le visiteur se déplace en tant qu'observateur. magma architecture a réussi cet effet en partie grâce à des formes amorphes qui permettent aux limites de l'espace de disparaître, ainsi qu'à travers les réflexions des couleur, des personnes, des maquettes et des dessins qui lui confèrent un éclat orange.

Il centro della mostra head in | im kopf è la scultura spaziale amorfa, progettata per i 150 m² dell'area espositiva speciale nella Berlinische Galerie. Tuffarsi nell'architettura dell'esposizione colorata di arancione significa per il visitatore appropriarsi attivamente della vita interna della scultura. Una esperienza nuova e sorprendente. Il colore nella mostra appare meno come una superficie avvolgente quanto una massa arancione, attraverso la quale ci si muove come osservatore. I magma architecture hanno raggiunto questo effetto parzialmente attraverso delle forme amorfe che fanno scomparire i confini della stanza, ma anche attraverso riflessi di colore, che donano alle persone, ai modelli e ai disegni una luce arancione.

MCBRIDE CHARLES RYAN
ARCHITECTURE + INTERIOR DESIGN | PRAHRAN, VIC, AUSTRALIA

Website   www.mcbridecharlesryan.com.au
Project   Templestowe Primary School Multipurpose Hall
Location   Templestowe, Australia
Year of Completion 2005
Building Materials Mixture of black fibre cement sheet cladding, brickwork,
                    semi-translucent sheet, and painted cladding
Color Specifications Paints: Dulux Weathershield X10 (Low Sheen)
                    Colors: Luck, Fiery glow, Polly, Jazzercise
Photo Credits   John Gollings, Melbourne

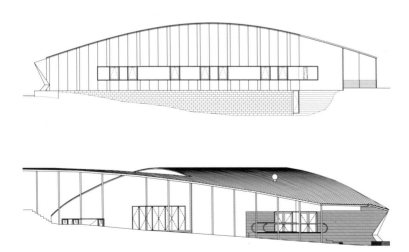

The primary school in Templestowe awakens memories: Generations of Australian students are familiar with the exercise books that have the Olympic stripes, which now also decorate the façade of the new multi-purpose hall. The hall had to be easily visible from the street and show its public use to visitors. The roof is arched like a parabola so that the interior offers enough space for performances and physical education. For the cladding of the façade, the architects McBride Charles Ryan mixed the materials—black and colorful metal panels alternate with masonry and semi-transparent panels in a striped form. On the inside, a large band of windows offers views of the surroundings.

Die Grundschule in Templestowe weckt Erinnerungen: Generationen von australischen Schülern kennen die Schreibhefte mit den olympischen Streifen, die auch die Fassade der neuen Mehrzweckhalle zieren. Die Halle sollte von der Straße aus gut sichtbar sein und den Besuchern die öffentliche Nutzung anzeigen. Das Dach ist wie eine Parabel gewölbt, so dass der Innenraum genug Platz für Vorführungen und für den Sportunterricht bietet. Für die Verkleidung der Fassade mischen die Architekten McBride Charles Ryan die Materialien – schwarze und farbige Metallpaneele wechseln sich mit Mauerwerk und semitransparenten Paneelen in Streifenform ab. Innen bietet ein großes Fensterband Aussichten in die Umgebung.

La escuela primaria de Templestowe trae viejos recuerdos. Son varias las generaciones de estudiantes australianos que evocarán los cuadernos con las bandas olímpicas, como las que decoran la fachada de la nueva sala multiusos. El pabellón ha de poderse distinguir con facilidad desde la calle y ha de mostrar su uso público a los visitantes. La cubierta está arqueada de forma parabólica, de modo que el interior dispone de espacio suficiente para representaciones y para las clases de educación física. Para recubrir la fachada, los arquitectos McBride Charles Ryan mezclaron materiales: paneles metálicos negros y coloridos se intercalan con mampostería y paneles semitransparentes con forma de tiras. Por el interior, una largo vano acristalado ofrece vistas a los alrededores.

L'école primaire de Templestowe réveille des souvenirs : des générations d'élèves australiens sont familiers des livres d'exercice ornés des lignes olympiques qui décorent maintenant la façade du hall polyvalent. Le hall devait être facilement visible depuis la rue et montrer son usage public aux visiteurs. Le toit est en forme d'arche comme une parabole, ainsi l'intérieur offre assez d'espace pour les diverses manifestations et l'éducation physique. Pour le revêtement de la façade, les architectes McBride Charles Ryan ont mélangé les matériaux – des panneaux de métal colorés et noirs alternent avec de la maçonnerie et des panneaux semi-transparent pour former des rayures. A l'intérieur, une large baie vitrée offre une vue sur les environs.

La scuola elementare a Templestowe risveglia i ricordi: generazioni di scolari australiani conoscono i quaderni con le righe olimpioniche che decorano anche la facciata della nuova sala polifunzionale. La sala doveva essere ben visibile dalla strada e mostrare ai visitatori l'utilizzo pubblico. Il tetto è inarcato come una parabola, così che l'area interna possa offrire sufficiente spazio per le rappresentazioni e per le lezioni di ginnastica. Per il rivestimento della facciata gli architetti McBride Charles Ryan hanno mischiato i materiali – pannelli di metallo neri e colorati si alternano con muratura e pannelli semitrasparenti a forma di righe. All'interno una grande finestra a nastro offre la vista sui dintorni.

MOTORPLAN ARCHITEKTUR+STADTPLANUNG | MANNHEIM, GERMANY

Website	www.motorplan.de
Project	Popakademie
Project's website	www.popakademie.de
Location	Mannheim, Germany
Year of Completion	2004
Building Materials	Structure: steel with metal stud and wood. Skin: Redwood, white polycarbonate corrugated sheets, and galvanized metal
Color Specification	Façade of stretched metal. Interiors and ceilings partially lacquered with high-gloss polish, red, different shades of gray, black, white. Interior: green
Photo Credits	Daniel Lukac

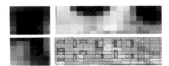

The Pop Academy, a new prototype of an "educational institution", has been given a progressive face through the choice of its façade materials and their graphics. Anodized stretched metal shimmers metallically in three shades with a simple and robust effect. The grids of the metal skin, which have been rotated by 90°, change their look in a chameleon-like way depending on the location and movement: sometimes they appear to be closed to the maximum degree and reveal the actual shades of the metal and sometimes they are transparent—as many-faceted as pop music itself. The graphic arrangement of the eloxal tones is based on a coarsely pixilated portrait of John Lennon. The interiors are determined by orange as the CI color of the academy. As a contrast, the ceilings, floors, and walls on the upper floor have been treated with high-gloss lacquer.

Die Popakademie, ein neuartiger Prototyp von „Lehranstalt", erhält durch die Wahl des Fassadenmaterials und deren Grafik ein progressives Gesicht. Eloxiertes Streckmetall schimmert metallisch in drei Farbtönen, wirkt einfach und robust. Die um 90° gedrehten Gitter der Metall-Haut wechseln chamäleonartig, je nach Standort und in der Bewegung, ihr Bild: mal wirkt sie maximal geschlossen und im eigentlichen Farbton des Metalls, mal transparent – so facettenreich wie Popmusik. Der grafischen Anordnung der Eloxaltöne liegt ein grob aufgepixeltes Portrait von John Lennon zu Grunde. Orange als CI-Farbe der Akademie bestimmt die Innenräume, als Kontrast wurden im Obergeschoss Decken, Böden und Wände in Blaugrün hochglanzlackiert.

La Popakademie (Academia pop), un innovador prototipo de "centro de enseñanza", cuenta con un fachada dinámica gracias a la elección del material de la misma. El metal desplegado anodizado produce destellos en tres colores y resulta sencillo al tiempo que robusto. El enrejado virado en 90º del revestimiento metálico tiene un efecto camaleónico dependiendo del punto de observación y del movimiento: puede parecer opaco, y en el propio color del metal, transparente, algo tan variado como la música pop. La disposición gráfica de los tonos anodizados conforma un retrato pixelado de John Lennon. El naranja, el color corporativo de la academia, domina los espacios interiores, mientras que el techo, el suelo y las paredes de la planta superior relucen en un verde azulado.

La Pop Academy, un nouveau prototype « d'institution éducative », a été dotée d'un visage progressif grâce au choix des matériaux de sa façade et leur graphisme. Le métal étiré anodisé miroite métalliquement dans l'ombre des arbres avec un effet simple et solide. Les grilles du revêtement métallique, qui ont tourné à 90°, change d'apparence comme un caméléon selon leur emplacement et leur mouvement : parfois ils paraissent fermés au maximum et révèlent les teintes réelles du métal et parfois elles sont transparentes – avec autant de facettes que la musique pop elle-même. L'agencement graphique des teintes Eloxal est basé sur un portrait grossièrement pixellisé de John Lennon. Les intérieurs sont caractérisés par la couleur orange, qui donne son identité à l'académie. En contraste, les plafonds, les sols et les murs de l'étage supérieur ont été traités avec une laque ultra-brillante.

La Popakademie, un nuovo prototipo di "istituto scolastico", riceve, grazie al materiale usato per la facciata e alla sua grafica, un aspetto progressista. Del metallo esteso anodizzato brilla in tre tonalità metalliche e appare semplice e robusto. Le grate della pelle di metallo, girate di 90°, cambiano in modo camaleontico, a seconda del punto di osservazione e al loro movimento: a volte appaiono chiuse al massimo e nell'effettiva tonalità del metallo, altre volte trasparenti – così sfaccettata come la musica pop. La disposizione grafica delle tonalità dell'anodizzazione si basa su un ritratto di John Lennon realizzato in pixel grossolani. L'arancione, in qualità di colore CI dell'accademia, definisce i locali interni, mentre come contrasto i soffitti, i pavimenti e le pareti del piano superiore sono stati laccati in blu-verde lucido.

NEUTELINGS RIEDIJK ARCHITECTEN | ROTTERDAM, NETHERLANDS

Website	www.neutelings-riedijk.com
Project	Netherlands Institute for Sound and Vision
Location	Mediapark, Hilversum, Netherlands
Year of Completion	2006
Building Materials	Glass, steel, concrete, aluminum (ceiling panels), slate, wooden wall and ceiling cladding, steel window frames
Color Specification	The images on the façade are shots of different Dutch TV shows. These shots were first converted into a CMYK color scheme (cyan, magenta, yellow, black). All black parts were converted into a 3D relief glass panel and the other three colors were printed on the glass
Photo Credits	Daria Scagliola, Stijn Brakkee

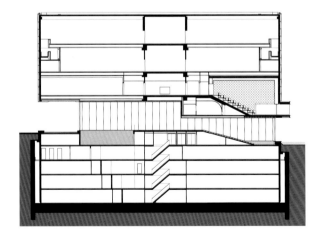

The **Netherlands Institute** for Sound and Vision is divided in half: The archive and storeroom for the entire audiovisual material that radio and television has produced in the Netherlands since their early days is located in a subterranean massif of greenish shimmering slate. Above the canyon, the public area connects the various uses and bridges lead across the "canyons." Reception halls, a restaurant, and a video auditorium are situated here next to a museum and rooms for offices and secondary uses. The façade is ingenious: Neutelings Riedijk Architecten translated 748 original television images into glass reliefs and united them into more than 2,100 glass panels.

Das Niederländische Institut für Ton und Bild ist zweigeteilt: In einem unterirdischen Massiv aus grünlich schimmerndem Schiefer finden sich Archive und Lager für das gesamte audiovisuelle Material, das Funk und Fernsehen seit ihren frühen Tagen in den Niederlanden produzierten. Über dem Canyon verbindet der öffentliche Bereich die unterschiedlichen Nutzungen, und Brücken führen über die „Schluchten". Rezeptionshalle, Restaurant und ein Video-Auditorium finden sich hier neben einem Museum und Räumen für Büros und Nebennutzungen. Die Fassade ist ausgeklügelt: Neutelings Riedijk Architecten übersetzten 748 originale Fernsehbilder in Glasreliefs, zusammengefasst in mehr als 2.100 Glaspaneelen.

El Instituto Holandés de Imagen y Sonido se divide en dos partes: en una gran mole subterránea de pizarra reflectante en tonos verdosos se encuentran los archivos y el almacén de material audiovisual – las primeras producciones holandesas de radio y televisión. La zona común comunica los diferentes usos mediante puentes que sobrevuelan un "cañón". La sala de recepción, el restaurante y un "vídeoauditorio" se sitúan junto a un museo y a los despachos para oficinas y usos secundarios. La fachada es una demostración de ingenio: los arquitectos de Neutelings Riedijk transformaron 748 imágenes de televisión originales en relieves de cristal, que luego fusionaron en más de 2.100 paneles.

L'institut Néerlandais de Son et de Vison est divisé en deux : un massif souterrain d'ardoise aux reflets verts abrite les archives et les réserves contenant tout le matériel audiovisuel que la radio et la télévision ont produit aux Pays-Bas depuis leurs premiers jours. Au-dessus du canyon, l'espace public relie les différentes utilisations et des ponts mènent de chaque côté des « canyons ». Des halls de réception, un restaurant et un auditorium vidéo sont situés près d'un musée et de bureaux et pièces secondaires. La façade est ingénieuse : les architectes de Neutelings Riedijk Architecten ont mis en relief 748 images de télévision pour les combiner sur plus de 2 100 panneaux de verre.

L'istituto olandese per il suono e l'immagine è diviso in due: in un blocco sotterraneo di ardesia splendente di verde si trovano gli archivi e i magazzini per l'intero materiale audiovisivo, che la radio e la televisione hanno prodotto nei Paesi Bassi fin dalle origini. Attraverso un canyon l'area pubblica unisce i diversi utilizzi e dei ponti portano attraverso le "gole". La sala della reception, il ristorante e un auditorium video si ritrovano qui accanto a un museo e ai locali per gli uffici e per utilizzi secondari. La facciata è raffinata: gli architetti Neutelings Riedijk hanno tradotto 748 immagini televisive originali in rilievi su vetro, riassunti in più di 2.100 pannelli di vetro.

NERVOUS IN THE SERVICE | SKIVE, DENMARK

Website	www.nervousintheservice.dk
Designers names	Stine Osther, Caroline Hansen, Mie Nielsen, Rikke K. Larsen
Project	Student Dormitory "Krabbesholm Art College"
Location	Krabbesholm, Denmark
Year of Completion	2007
Building Materials	Wooden boxes spray-painted at a car bodyshop
Color Specifications	Multifacetted monochromacity: the project explores the ranges within one color: different shades and their influences on each other
Photo Credits	Laura Stamer, www.laurastamer.dk

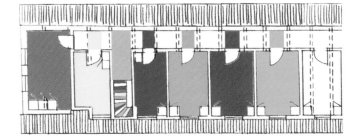

Art students feel good in the student dormitory of the Krabbesholm Art College by Nervous in the Service. The project "Home Sweet Color" is characterized by rooms designed in mono-colors. Brown, yellow, green, red, grey and blue—depending upon the size of the room, the colors have various intensities of nuances. The yellow student room is the smallest—and almost monochrome. On the other hand, in the red room—the largest—the range is spread from orange to purple. The monochrome variety makes every room into an individual home. The architects relied less on the psychological bag of tricks and more on the experiences from textile and fashion design for the color scheme.

Im Studentenwohnheim „Krabbesholm Art College" von Nervous in the Service fühlen sich Kunststudenten wohl. Das Projekt „Home Sweet Color" zeichnet sich durch die einfarbig angelegten Räume aus. Braun, Gelb, Grün, Rot, Grau und Blau – je nach Größe des Raumes sind die Farben verschieden stark nuanciert. Das gelbe Studentenzimmer ist das kleinste – und fast monochrom. Im roten Zimmer, dem größten, wird hingegen der Fächer von Orange bis hin zu Purpur aufgespannt. Die „monochrome Vielfalt" macht aus jedem Zimmer ein individuelles Zuhause. Bei der Farbgebung greifen die Architektinnen weniger auf die psychologische Trickkiste zurück, als mehr auf Erfahrungen aus dem Textil- und Modedesign.

Los estudiantes de arte se sienten como en casa en la residencia de estudiantes de la Escuela de Arte de Krabbesholm diseñada por Nervous in the Service. El proyecto "Home Sweet Color" se caracteriza por sus estancias monocromáticas. Marrón, amarillo, verde, rojo, gris y azul en sus distintos tonos son los colores de las habitaciones según su tamaño. La más pequeña es la amarilla, casi monocromática. La roja - la más grande - abarca tonos que van del naranja al púrpura. La "diversidad monocromática" convierte cada cuarto en un verdadero hogar. A la hora de determinar los colores, los arquitectos no se basaron tanto en cuestiones psicológicas, sino más bien en la experiencia en el diseño de textiles y moda.

Les étudiants en art se sentent bien dans le dortoir du Krabbesholm Art College, conçu par Nervous in the Service. Le projet « Home Sweet Color » est caractérisé par des pièces d'une seule couleur. Marron, jaune, vert, rouge, gris et bleu – selon la taille de la pièce, les couleurs offrent diverses intensités de nuances. La chambre d'étudiant jaune est la plus petite – et elle est quasiment monochrome. Mais dans la chambre rouge – la plus grande – la gamme s'étend de l'orange au violet. La variété des monochromes fait de chaque chambre une maison particulière. Les architectes se sont moins appuyés sur le bric-à-brac psychologique que sur leur expérience du textile et de la mode pour l'agencement des couleurs.

Nel collegio per studenti di "Krabbesholm Art College" di Nervous in the Service gli studenti d'arte si trovano bene. Il progetto "Home Sweet Color" si caratterizza per le stanze in colori a tinta unita. Marrone, giallo, verde, rosso, grigio e blu – a seconda della grandezza della stanza i colori sono stati sfumati più o meno fortemente. La camera studentesca gialla è la più piccola – e quasi monocromatica. Nella camera rossa, la più grande, invece la gamma presentata va dall'arancione fino alla porpora. La "molteplicità monocromatica" rende ogni camera una casa individuale. Per l'assegnazione del colore le signore architetti hanno fatto meno riferimento ai trucchi psicologici quanto alle esperienze fatte nel design tessile e di moda.

PANORAMA INTERNATIONAL LTD. | HONG KONG, HONG KONG

Website	www.panoramahk.com
Project	Blue One Club
Location	Shenzhen, China
Year of Completion	2004
Building Materials	Glass, stainless steel, fabrics
Color Specifications	Blue, black
Photo Credits	Courtesy of PANORAMA International Ltd., Hong Kong

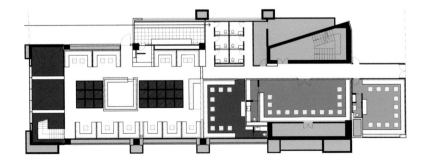

Music meets architecture in Hong Kong: The Blue One, a dance-club label, has been realized at the location of the same name with Panorama International. Visitors will find bars, dance floors, and VIP rooms on two floors. The interior illustrates the power of illusion and the uniqueness of blue, which is intended to create the perfect chill-out experience for guests. The interplay of light, sound, and music gives the place a lively urban feeling. The very sparsely furnished rooms, immersed in blue light that is further intensified by luminous objects, alternate with glass dance floors. The clearness of the color blue and the spartan feel of the design create the visual and psychological stimulus.

Musik trifft Architektur in Hongkong: das Blue One, ein Dance Club Label, realisiert mit Panorama International die gleichnamige Location. Auf zwei Stockwerken finden die Besucher Bars, Tanzflächen und VIP-Räume. Das Interieur setzt auf die Kraft der Illusion und die Einzigartigkeit von Blau, die den Gästen das perfekte Chill-Out-Erlebnis verschaffen soll. Das Zusammenspiel von Licht, Klängen und Musik gibt dem Ort etwas urban-lebendiges. Die sehr reduziert möblierten Räume, in blaues Licht getaucht, das von Leuchtobjekten noch verstärkt wird, wechseln sich ab mit verglasten Tanzflächen. Das Klare der Farbe Blau und die spartanische Anmutung des Designs machen den visuellen und psychologischen Reiz aus.

La música y la arquitectura se funden en Hong Kong: el Blue One, un sello de "dance-club", ha ejecutado junto a Panorama International el local del mismo nombre. Los que lo visiten encontrarán en dos plantas bares, pistas de baile y reservados VIP. El interior manifiesta el poder de la ilusión y la exclusividad a través del azul, pretendiendo con él crear toda una experiencia chill-out para los clientes. La combinación de luz, sonido y música permite sentir lo que significa vivir en la ciudad. Los espacios, con escaso mobiliario y sumergidos en una luz azulada intensificada mediante luminarias, se alternan con pistas de baile con suelo de cristal. La claridad del azul y el diseño espartano sirven de estímulo visual y psicológico.

La musique rencontre l'architecture à Hongkong : le club-dance The Blue One a été construit à l'endroit du même nom par Panorama International. Les visiteurs y trouveront des bars, des pistes de danse et des salons VIP sur deux étages. L'intérieur illustre le pouvoir de l'illusion et l'aspect unique du bleu, avec pour but d'offrir une parfaite expérience rafraîchissante aux clients. Le jeu entre la lumière, le son et la musique confère au lieu un feeling urbain intense. Les pièces meublées avec parcimonie, immergées dans une lumière bleue encore intensifiée par des objets lumineux, alternent avec les pistes de danse en verre. La clarté de la couleur bleue et l'aspect spartiate du design créent des stimuli visuels et psychologiques.

La musica incontra l'architettura a Hong Kong: il Blue One, un Dance Club Label, realizza con la Panorama International la location con lo stesso nome. Su due piani i visitatori trovano dei bar, delle piste da ballo e delle sale VIP. L'interno punta sulla forza dell'illusione e sull'unicità del blu, che procurerà agli ospiti la perfetta esperienza Chill-Out. L'interazione di luce, suoni e musica regala al luogo un qualcosa di urbano-vivo. Le stanze con una mobilia molto ridotta, affondata in luce blu che viene rafforzata ulteriormente da oggetti illuminati, si alterna con piste da ballo vetrate. La chiarezza del colore blu e la pretesa spartana del design costituiscono il fascino visivo e psicologico.

PANORAMA INTERNATIONAL LTD. | HONG KONG, HONG KONG

Website	www.panoramahk.com
Project	California Red Box Re-branding
Location	Guangzhou, China
Year of Completion	2006
Building Materials	Red spray paint, metal plate, stainless steel, plastic board, leather, back coated glass & LED
Color Specifications	Red, charcoal grey, different shades of grey
Photo Credits	Courtesy of PANORAMA International Ltd., Hong Kong

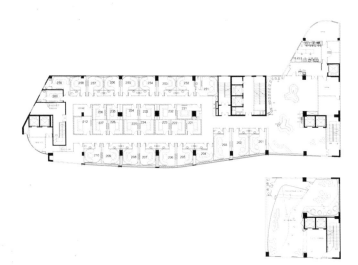

Karaoke, a Japanese invention of the 1980s, is now the dominating form of entertainment in Asia. Panorama International dedicates its design completely to the unique experience of "live singing with musical accompaniment." The California Red Box Karaoke in Guangzhou puts the guests in the right mood for pop songs: Variations of grey and magenta tones make up the main colors and convey the feeling of being completely enveloped. Above all, magenta—with its feminine touch—should appeal to the club's new target group: women. Glossy and matte wall and ceiling cladding creates a mystical reality in which anyone can act out the illusion of being a star.

Karaoke, eine japanische Erfindung der 80er Jahre, ist heute die dominierende Form von Entertainment in Asien. Panorama International stellen ihr Design ganz in den Dienst der einzigartigen Erfahrung des „live singing mit Musikbegleitung". Die California Red Box Karaoke in Guangzhou versetzt die Gäste in die richtige Stimmung für Popsongs: Variationen von Grau- und Magentatönen bilden die Leitfarben und vermitteln das Gefühl, ganz umhüllt zu sein. Vor allem Magenta, mit seinem femininen Touch, soll die neue Zielgruppe des Clubs ansprechen: Frauen. Glänzende und matte Wand- und Deckenverkleidungen schaffen eine mystische Wirklichkeit, in der jede(r) die Illusion ausleben kann, ein Star zu sein.

El karaoke, un invento japonés de los años ochenta, es en la actualidad la principal forma de entretenimiento en Asia. Panorama International consagra su diseño por completo a la experiencia insuperable que supone "cantar en directo con acompañamiento musical". El Karaoke California Red Box de Guangzhou consigue crear el ambiente idóneo para la música pop. Variaciones que van del gris al magenta componen la paleta principal y la sensación envolvente es total. El magenta, con su toque femenino, se dirige principalmente los nuevos clientes potenciales del club: las mujeres. Los revestimientos refulgentes y mates en paredes y techos crean una realidad un tanto mística en la que cualquiera puede llegar a creerse una estrella.

Le karaoké, une invention japonaise des années 80, est actuellement la forme de loisirs dominante en Asie. Panorama International consacre tout son art du design à cette expérience unique de « chant en direct avec accompagnement musical ». Le California Red Box Karaoké à Guangzhou met les clients dans l'humeur idéale pour les chansons pop : une variation sur les tons gris et magenta constitue le thème de couleur principal et apporte une sensation d'enveloppement total. Le magenta surtout – avec sa touche féminine – devrait attirer le nouveau groupe cible du club : les femmes. Le revêtement brillant et mat des murs et des plafonds crée une réalité mystique dans laquelle chacun peut avoir l'illusion d'être une star.

Il karaoke, una invenzione giapponese degli anni '80, è oggigiorno la forma dominante di intrattenimento in Asia. La Panorama International mette a disposizione il suo design completamente al servizio di questa esperienza unica nel suo genere del "live singing con accompagnamento musicale". La California Red Box Karaoke a Guangzhou crea per i suoi ospiti la giusta atmosfera per le canzoni pop: delle variazioni di grigio e magenta formano i colori guida e trasmettono la sensazione di essere completamente avvolti. Soprattutto il colore magenta, con il suo tocco femminile, ha lo scopo di rivolgersi al nuovo target del Club: le donne. I rivestimenti delle pareti e dei soffitti lucidi e opachi creano una realtà mistica, nella quale ognuna/o può vivere l'illusione di essere una star.

PANORAMA INTERNATIONAL LTD. | HONG KONG, HONG KONG

Website   www.panoramahk.com
Project   Restaurant Golden Dynasty
Location   Hong Kong, Hong Kong
Year of Completion 2004
Building Materials Glass, timber, leather, plaster and bamboo
Color Specifications Blue, gray
Photo Credits   Courtesy of PANORAMA International Ltd., Hong Kong

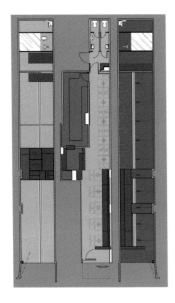

Dining in harmony with yin and yang: Chinese cuisine is served at the Restaurant Golden Dynasty in the center of Hong Kong. The architects of Panorama International rely on tradition and modern style in relation to each other in the design, resulting in an identity for the Golden Dynasty brand. The yin and yang principle is clearly reflected in the color concept: Gray cement finds its counterpart in the violet paint and indirect blue light is softened and becomes warmer through the red lamps. The experience of the room is completed by a bamboo construction. It almost appears to be floating because of the material and color scheme, reminiscent of nature as it shields the guests from the outer world.

Dinieren im Einklang mit Yin und Yang: Im Restaurant Golden Dynasty im Zentrum von Hongkong wird zeitgemäße, chinesische Küche serviert. Die Architekten von Panorama International setzen Tradition und Moderne im Design zueinander in Beziehung und geben damit der Marke Golden Dynasty eine Identität. Das Yin und Yang Prinzip spiegelt sich deutlich im Farbkonzept wider: Grauer Zement findet seinen Gegenpol im violetten Anstrich, indirektes, blaues Licht wird durch rote Lampen durchbrochen und wärmer. Das Raumerlebnis wird komplettiert durch eine Bambuskonstruktion. Diese scheint fast zu schweben, durch das Material und die an Natur erinnernde Farbgebung schirmt sie die Gäste von der Außenwelt ab.

Cenar en armonía con el Yin y el Yang: En el restaurante Golden Dynasty del centro de Hong Kong se sirve comida china contemporánea. Los arquitectos de Panorama International han apoyado su diseño en una relación entre tradición y modernidad, dándole así una identidad a la marca Golden Dinasty. El principio del Yin y el Yang se refleja de forma palmaria en el concepto cromático: el cemento gris encuentra su opuesto en la pintura violeta; la luz azul indirecta se hace más suave y cálida mediante luminarias rojas. El diseño del local se completa con una construcción en bambú, que parece estar flotando gracias a unos materiales y unos colores con reminiscencias naturales que protegen a los comensales del mundo exterior.

Dîner en harmonie avec le yin et le yang : le restaurant Golden Dynasty sert de la cuisine chinoise au centre de Hongkong. Les architectes de Panorama International se basent sur une interaction entre la tradition et le style moderne pour le design, et donnent une identité à la marque Golden Dynasty. Le principe du yin et du yang est clairement illustré dans le concept des couleurs : le ciment gris trouve sa contrepartie dans la peinture violette et la lumière bleue indirecte est adoucie et plus chaude grâce aux lampes rouges. L'expérience vécue dans la pièce est complétée par une construction en bambou. Elle paraît presque flotter en raison de ses matériaux et de l'agencement des couleurs, qui rappellent la nature tout en protégeant les clients du monde extérieur.

Cenare in armonia con lo Yin e lo Yang: nel ristorante Golden Dynasty nel centro di Hong Kong si servono dei piatti della cucina contemporanea cinese. Gli architetti della Panorama International uniscono la tradizione e la modernità nel design e danno così una identità al marchio Golden Dynasty. Il principio dello Yin e dello Yang si rispecchia chiaramente nel concetto del colore: Del cemento grigio trova la sua contraparte nella pittura viola, della luce indiretta blu viene spezzata e riscaldata da lampade rosse. L'esperienza dell'ambiente viene completata da una costruzione di bambù. Questa sembra quasi volare; grazie al materiale e alla colorazione che ricorda la natura protegge gli ospiti dal mondo esterno.

PLANUNGSGEMEINSCHAFT RHEINUFER
FISCHTORPLATZ – KAISERTORPLATZ | MAINZ, GERMANY

Architects	Planquadrat Elfers Geskes Krämer Part. G. dwb BDA
	Architects+Urban Planners	Darmstadt, Germany
	IBC Ingenieurbau-Consult GmbH	Mainz, Germany
Landscape Architects	Bierbaum.Aichele.landschaftsarchitekten BDLA / dwb	
	Mainz, Germany
Statics, Electricity	IBC Ingenieurbau-Consult GmbH	Mainz, Germany
Websites	www.planquadrat.com, www.ingenieurbau-consult.de,
	www.bierbaumaichele.de
Project	Rheinufergarage Mainz
Location	Mainz, Germany
Year of Completion	2004
Building Materials	Concrete, epoxy floor coating
Color Specifications	Complementary play of color – red and green
Photo Credits	Christoph Kraneburg, Cologne

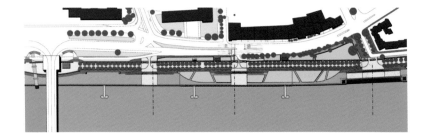

The planning alliance turned the wish of involved citizens into reality: An area of the Rhine bank with a high quality of life should be car-free. What was previously a parking lot is now a greenbelt recreation area—the garage on the bank of the Rhine makes this possible. A green landscape with 35 sycamore trees and lawns in various geometric forms was created on the roof of the building. On the parking levels, the floor is covered by a bright, fresh green. The intention is to continue the newly laid-out above-ground green landscape underground. A corresponding red, analogous to the red sandstone of the castle building, has been used for the exit to the castle side. The exit to the library—which is again green—continues the complementary color play.

Die Planungsgemeinschaft setzte den Wunsch engagierter Bürger innerhalb des Rheinuferforums um: ein hochwertiger Rhein-Uferbereich sollte autofrei werden. Was früher Parkplatz war, ist jetzt Naherholungsgebiet - die Rheinufergarage macht das möglich. Auf dem Dach des Baus entstand eine grüne Landschaft mit 35 Platanen und Rasenflächen in unterschiedlichen geometrischen Formen. In den Parkgeschossen ist der Boden in hellem, frischem Grün beschichtet. Die neu angelegte, oberirdische Grünfläche soll sich unterirdisch fortsetzen. Für den Ausgang zur Schlossseite wurde ein entsprechendes Rot eingesetzt, analog zum roten Sandstein der Schlossbebauung. Der Ausgang zur Bibliothek, wiederum in Grün, führt das Komplementärfarbspiel weiter.

La comunidad de planificación plasmó los deseos de unos ciudadanos comprometidos: un área de gran calidad en la ribera del Rin debía quedar libre de coches. Lo que antes era un aparcamiento, es hoy una zona de descanso. El Garaje de la Ribera de Rin (Rheinufergarage) lo ha hecho posible. En la azotea se creo una zona verde con 35 plataneros y zonas con césped de diferentes formas geométricas. El pavimento de las plantas de aparcamiento es de un verde claro y fresco. La nueva zona verde sobre nivel continuará en el subterráneo. La salida al castillo se ha marcado en rojo, de forma similar a la arenisca rojiza del propio castillo. La salida a la biblioteca, de nuevo en verde, continúa con la combinación cromática complementaria.

La communauté de la planification a réalisé le rêve des citoyens engagés : une zone de la berge du Rhin, avec une grande qualité de vie, sera désormais interdite aux voitures. Ce qui était précédemment un parking est maintenant un espace de loisirs vert – grâce au parking sur la berge du Rhin. Un paysage vert planté de 35 platanes et de pelouses de formes géométriques diverses a été créé sur le toit du bâtiment. A chaque étage du parking, le sol est couvert d'un vert acidulé. L'objectif est de prolonger sous terre le paysage vert récemment aménagé au-dessus. Un rouge analogue au grès rouge du bâtiment du château a été utilisé pour la sortie côté château. La sortie vers la bibliothèque – qui est elle aussi verte – prolonge le jeu des couleurs élémentaires.

La comunità di progettazione ha realizzato il desiderio dei cittadini impegnati: la pregiata area della sponda del Reno diventerà zona pedonale. Quello che un tempo era un parcheggio ora è un'area relax - il garage sulla sponda del Reno lo rende possibile. Sul tetto della costruzione è stato creato un paesaggio verde con 35 platani e superfici erbose con differenti forme geometriche. Nei piani del parcheggio il pavimento è stato rivestito di un verde chiaro e fresco. L'area verde in superficie appena progettata proseguirà nel sotterraneo. Per l'uscita al lato del castello è stato usato un rosso corrispondente, analogo alla pietra arenaria della costruzione dell'edificio. L'uscita alla biblioteca invece è verde e prosegue questo gioco dei colori complementari.

RMJM HONG KONG LTD. | HONG KONG, HONG KONG

Website	www.rmjm.com
Project	Centralised Science Laboratories building at The Chinese University of Hong Kong
Location	Hong Kong, Hong Kong
Year of Completion	2004
Building Materials	Multi-layered laminated colored glass, concrete, steel, aluminum louvres, granite tiling
Color Specifications	The curving façade is composed of multi-layered laminated glass, designed around the periodic table of elements. Random swatches and lines of clear, yellow, orange, green, red and blue tones create a dynamic internal environment and externally reflect the ideas of the building's function.
Photo Credits	Graham Uden

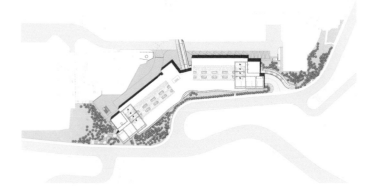

An icon nestled into the hilly landscape, the Centralised Science Laboratories Building sits on the campus grounds of the Chinese University of Hong Kong offering great views of the Hong Kong Tolo Harbour. The concept for the laboratories building is based on the periodic table of elements. The RMJM HK designers translated the table into the structure's glass façade expressing the importance of the building as "high-tech experimental laboratories". The glass façade displays multi-layered laminated glass to create a series of colors that change with the time of day. The structure houses over 70 labs for the scientific and medical facilities.

Ein Symbol schmiegt sich in die hügelige Landschaft, das Gebäude auf dem Campusgelände selbst bietet eine tolle Aussicht auf den Tolo Hafen von Hongkong. Als Idee hinter dem Laborgebäude der Chinesischen Universität steht das Periodensystem der Elemente aus der Chemie, das die Planer von RMJM HK Architekten in eine Glasfassade übersetzten. Diese nimmt Bezug auf die Geschichte des Gebäudes als ein „Hochsicherheits-Laboratorium", in dem mehr als 70 Labore für die wissenschaftlichen und medizinischen Fakultäten Raum fürs Experiment finden – das Experimentelle visualisiert die Fassade: einige der Glasflächen sind laminiert, so dass ein System von verschiedenen Farb-Elementen entsteht.

Todo un icono apostado en un escarpado paisaje. El edificio central de los laboratorios de Ciencias está ubicado en el campus de la Universidad de Hong Kong, y ofrece una maravillosa vista al puerto de Tolo. El concepto del que parte este edificio es la tabla periódica de elementos. Los proyectistas de RMJM HK la tradujeron en una fachada acristalada para expresar la importancia del edificio como "laboratorio experimental de tecnología punta". La fachada cuenta con cristales laminados multicapa que generan diferentes colores según la hora del día. Esta edificación alberga más de 70 laboratorios a disposición de las facultades de Ciencia y Medicina.

Icône nichée dans un paysage vallonné, le bâtiment des Laboratoires de Science Centralisés est situé sur le campus de l'Université Chinoise de Hongkong, avec une magnifique vue sur le Port Tolo de la ville. Le concept du bâtiment des laboratoires est basé sur le tableau périodique des éléments. Les designers de RMJM HK l'ont interprété dans la façade de verre de la structure, exprimant l'importance du bâtiment en tant que laboratoire d'expérience high-tech. La façade de verre affiche plusieurs couches de verre feuilleté pour créer un ensemble de couleurs qui changent selon l'heure du jour. La structure abrite plus de 70 labos pour les installations scientifiques et médicales.

Un'icona annidata nel paesaggio collinare, l'edificio dei Centralized Science Laboratories è situato nell'area del campus della Chinese University di Hong Kong e offre una grande veduta del porto Tolo di Hong Kong. Il concetto dell'edificio dei laboratori è basato sulla tavola periodica degli elementi. I designer RMJM HK hanno tradotto la tabella nella facciata di vetro della struttura ed hanno espresso l'importanza dell'edificio in quanto dei "laboratori sperimentali di high-tech". La facciata di vetro presenta del vetro laminato multi-strato che crea una serie di colori che cambiano nell'arco della giornata. La struttura ospita più di 70 laboratori per le attrezzature scientifiche e mediche.

SAIA BARBARESE TOPOUZANOV ARCHITECTES | MONTREAL (QC), CANADA
AEDIFICA INC. | MONTREAL (QC), CANADA

Website	www.sbt.qc.ca
	www.aedifica.com
Project	Montreal Convention Centre Expansion
Location	Montreal (QC), Canada
Year of Completion	2003
Building Materials	Colored glass, steel: north and west façades. Stone: east and south façades
Color Specification	Glazing colors: red, yellow, blue, orange, green, purple. Interior neutral colors: gray, white, metallic, black (in various textures). Pink 'Lipstick Forest'
Photo Credits	Marc Cramer

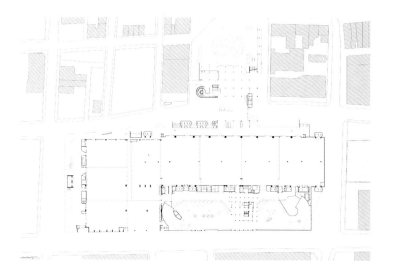

The Convention Center situated at the edge of Old Montreal serves as a portal to the modern city. SBT Architectes responded with a colorful solution: a prismatic building skin, radiating warmth inside and out. During the day, a multitude of hues flood the interior and immerse the public in a world of fantasy; at night the illuminating façade brightens the urban landscape. Light diffused in varying intensities through this glazed filter, coupled with reflective mirrored surfaces, enlivens the white winter days. Announcing arrival, large expanses of monochrome tones mark points of street entry, while a varied palette renders the interior spaces distinct. Exhibition areas are toned-down and areas of movement and gathering are bathed in color in contrast to the grey-toned granite floor.

Das an das alte Montreal angrenzende Convention Center dient als Portal zur modernen Stadt. Die SBT Architectes antworten darauf mit einer farbenfrohen Lösung: Eine Gebäudefassade in Regenbogenfarben, strahlende Wärme innen und außen. Tagsüber durchfluten zahlreiche Farbschattierungen den Innenraum und tauchen den Öffentlichkeitsbereich in eine bunte Phantasiewelt, abends erhellt die erleuchtete Fassade den städtischen Raum. Gepaart mit reflektierenden, spiegelnden Oberflächen belebt das durch diesen Glasfilter unterschiedlich intensiv gestreute Licht die weißen Wintertage. Die Ankunft ankündigend, markieren großzügige Felder in monochromatischen Tönen die Punkte, wo eine Straße auf das Gebäude trifft, während eine abwechslungsreiche Palette den Innenbereich prägt. Die Ausstellungsbereiche sind abgetönt und die Bewegungs- und Versammlungsflächen in Farbe getaucht als Kontrast zu dem graufarbigen Granitboden.

El Centro de Convenciones de Montreal, situado junto a la Vieja Montreal, ejerce de puerta de entrada a la ciudad moderna. Los arquitectos de SBT dieron respuesta con una solución de lo más colorista: una fachada con los colores del arco iris que irradia calor al interior y al exterior. De día, multitud de matices inundan el interior y sumergen el espacio público en un mundo de fantasía. Por la noche, la fachada encendida ilumina el paisaje urbano. La luz se difunde con intensidad variable a través de los filtros de cristal que van unidos a las superficies reflectantes de espejo, lo que llena de vida los días de invierno. Para anunciar la llegada, unas grandes superficies con tonos monocromáticos marcan los puntos que llevan de la calle al edificio, mientras que una paleta muy variada inunda el espacio interior. Las áreas expositivas tienen colores más tenues en comparación a las zonas de paso y reunión, con más color en contraste con el pavimento de granito grisáceo.

Le Centre de Convention, situé en bordure du Vieux Montréal, sert de portail à la ville moderne. Les architectes de SBT ont réagi avec une proposition colorée : un revêtement prismatique, rayonnant de chaleur à l'intérieur et à l'extérieur. Pendant la journée, une multitude de teintes inondent l'intérieur et immergent le public dans un monde fantastique : la nuit, la façade illuminée éclaire le paysage urbain. La lumière est diffusée en différentes intensités à travers ce filtre glacé, accompagnée de surfaces miroir réfléchissantes, anime les blancs jours d'hiver. Annonçant les arrivées, de larges extensions de couleurs monochromes indiquent les points d'entrée, alors qu'une palette variée différencie les espaces intérieurs. Les zones d'exposition ont des couleurs plus douces, les zones de mouvement et de rassemblement sont baignées de couleur, en contraste avec le sol de granit gris.

Il Convention Center, che confina con la vecchia Montreal, serve da portale verso la città moderna. Gli architetti della SBT hanno dato una risposta con una soluzione ricca di colori: Una facciata del palazzo nei colori dell'arcobaleno, un calore irradiante, dentro e fuori. Durante il giorno numerose sfumature di colore attraversano lo spazio interno e affondano l'area pubblica in un mondo fantastico colorato, la sera la facciata illuminata rischiara la zona della città. La luce, che viene guidata tramite questo filtro di vetro in vario modo intensivo, ravviva le giornate bianche dell'inverno, in coppia con delle superfici riflettenti e a specchio. Annunciando l'arrivo, dei campi generosi segnano in toni monocromatici i punti attraverso i quali la strada incontra l'edificio, mentre una gamma variopinta imprime l'area interna. Le zone dell'esposizione sono smorzate e le superfici di movimento e riunione sono tinte di colori, come contrasto con il pavimento di granito grigio.

SAIA BARBARESE TOPOUZANOV ARCHITECTES | MONTREAL (QC), CANADA
MENKÈS SHOONER DAGENAIS LÉTOURNEUX ARCHITECTES | MONTREAL (QC), CANADA
LES ARCHITECTES DESNOYERS MERCURE ET ASSOCIÉS | MONTREAL (QC), CANADA

Website	www.sbt.qc.ca
	www.msdl.ca
	www.dma-arch.com
Project	Lassonde Building, École Polytechnique de Montreal
	(School of Engineering)
Website	www.polymtl.ca/lassonde
Location	Montreal (QC), Canada
Year of Completion	2005
Building Materials	Glass, brick
Color Specification	Red (the core of the earth), ochre (the ground), green (vegetation),
	blue (the sky)
Photo Credits	Alain Laforest, Marc Cramer, Guy Lavigueur, Frederic Saia

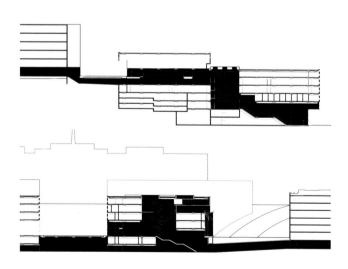

The Lassonde Building at the University of Montreal's École Polytechnique was aimed to achieve LEED Gold status. Inspired by this criteria, SBT architects looked at the earth's stratosphere to establish a color-coded strategy for the architectural concept. The scheme weaves together two roles for the colors: symbolic and programmatic. The colors red, ochre, green and blue symbolize respectively: earth's core, ground, vegetation and sky. Programmatically, red is associated with gathering spaces such as the auditoria and classrooms, ochre defines the computer sciences section, while the electrical department is rendered green and the library blue. Nuances in tone and intensity further distinguish public and private areas and set the mood: the atrium radiates intensive energy while the workrooms relay a quiet ambience.

Das Lassonde-Gebäude der zur University of Montreal gehörigen École Polytechnique wurde mit dem Ziel geplant, den LEED Gold Status zu erhalten. Inspiriert von diesem Kriterium warfen die SBT Architekten einen Blick auf die Erdstratosphäre, um eine farbcodierte Strategie für das architektonische Konzept zu kreieren. Das Schema zeigt zwei Farbebenen: Symbolisch und programmatisch. Die Farben Rot, Ocker, Grün und Blau symbolisieren dementsprechend: Den Erdkern, Boden, Vegetation und Himmel. Programmatisch ordnen sie Rot den Aufenthaltsbereichen zu, wie dem Auditorium und den Klassenräumen, Ocker bestimmt den Informatik-Bereich, während die Elektrotechnik in grün und die Bibliothek in blau gestaltet wird. Darüber hinaus nehmen die Planer eine Farbabstufung unterschiedlicher Intensität von öffentlichen zu privaten Bereichen vor und legen dadurch die Stimmung fest: Das Atrium strahlt eine intensive Energie aus, während die Arbeitsräume ein ruhiges Ambiente haben.

El edificio Lassonde en la École Polytechnique de la Universidad de Montreal tenía por objeto conseguir el nivel "LEED Gold". Siguiendo este criterio, los arquitectos de SBT se fijaron en la estratosfera para establecer una estrategia basada en un código de colores para crear su concepto arquitectónico. El esquema presenta dos niveles cromáticos: el simbólico y el programático. Rojo, ocre, verde y azul simbolizan respectivamente el núcleo de la Tierra, el suelo, la vegetación y el cielo. El rojo, como color programático, se destina a zonas de reunión como el auditorio o las aulas; el ocre determina las salas de informática; el verde define la electrotecnia, mientras que la biblioteca es azul. Los diseñadores utilizaron la gradación cromática para distinguir las zonas privadas de las públicas y constataron que el atrio transmitía una energía muy intensa, mientras que las áreas de trabajo disfrutaban de un ambiente relajado.

Le bâtiment Lassonde de l'Ecole Polytechnique de l'Université de Montréal se devait d'obtenir le statut LEED Or. Inspirés par ce critère, les architectes de SBT ont contemplé la stratosphère pour établir une stratégie de codes couleurs pour le concept architectural. L'agencement relie les deux rôles des couleurs : symbolique et programmatique. Les couleurs rouge, ocre, vert et bleu symbolisent respectivement : le noyau de la Terre, la terre, la végétation et le ciel. Par programme, le rouge est associé aux espaces de rassemblement comme les auditoriums et les salles de classe, l'ocre définit la section informatique, alors que le département électricité est caractérisé par le vert et la bibliothèque par le bleu. Les nuances de ton et d'intensité différencient davantage les espaces privés et publics et définissent l'ambiance : l'atrium dégage une énergie intense alors que les salles de classe offrent une ambiance calme.

L'edificio Lassonde che appartiene alla École Polytechnique della University of Montreal è stato pianificato con l'obiettivo di ricevere il LEED Gold Status. Ispirati da questo criterio, gli architetti della SBT hanno gettato uno sguardo sulla stratosfera terrestre per creare una strategia codificata di colore per il concetto architettonico. Lo schema mostra due livelli di colore: quello simbolico e quello programmatico. I colori rosso, ocra, verde e blu simboleggiano relativamente: il nucleo terrestre, il terreno, la vegetazione e il cielo. In senso programmatico associano il rosso alle zone di soggiorno come l'auditorium e le classi, l'ocra definisce la zona informatica, mentre quella elettrotecnica è realizzata in verde e la biblioteca in blu. Inoltre i progettisti hanno elaborato una gradazione di colori di varia intensità dalle zone pubbliche a quelle private e hanno così definito l'atmosfera: l'atrio emana un'energia intensa, mentre le stanze di lavoro presentano un ambiente tranquillo.

SKSK ARCHITECTS | BEIJING, CHINA

Website	www.sksk.cn
Project	Felissimo2
Location	Beijing, China
Year of Completion	2006
Building Materials	Floor with dust-proof oil paint finish, wall with lumber core backing, plasterboard water paint finish. Holes on walls and floor made of shopwork metal, green acrylic plate on the surface, stainless pipe baking painted green
Color Specifications	Green color simply implies 'nature'—this fashion brand has series of clothes made from natural materials, very comfortable and relaxing
Photo Credits	Seiichi Aoki (Beijing NDC Studio, Inc.), Beijing

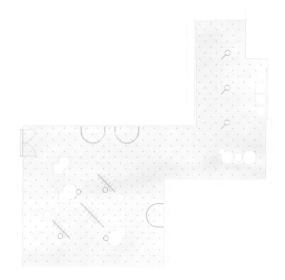

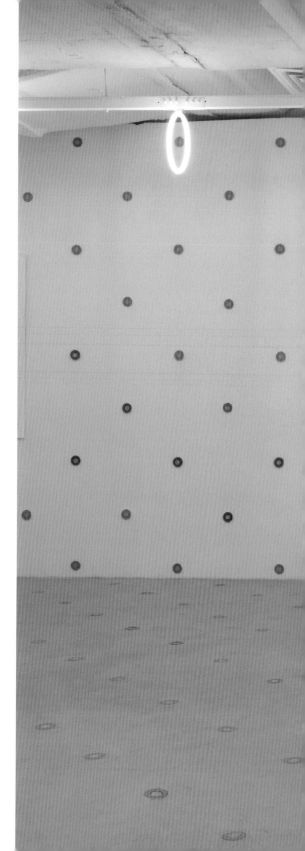

The fashion boutique Felissimo2 in Bcijing has green polka dots. Up to 1,000 dots are distributed over the walls and the floor, but they serve more than just the purpose of decoration. The entire concept has a system: A hole is hidden behind each of the dots. The matching plug-ins are attached to all of the pieces of furniture and decoration elements: clothing hooks, poles, tables, shelves, and flower vases. This results in a variety of possibilities for presenting the merchandise. The SKSK architects came up with another highlight: The principle of "plug-in" and "pit" does not just work symbolically: Some of the holes are attached to the power supply so that lighting elements can be inserted in them.

Die Modeboutique Felissimo2 in Peking ist grün gepunktet. Über den Wänden und den Fußboden verteilen sich bis zu 1.000 Punkte, die nicht allein zur Dekoration dienen. Das Ganze hat System: hinter jedem Punkt versteckt sich ein Loch. Die passenden Stecker sind an allen Möbelstücken und Dekorationselementen angebracht: Kleiderhaken, Stangen, Tische, Schränke, Blumenvasen. Auf diese Weise ergibt sich eine Vielzahl von Möglichkeiten, die Ware zu präsentieren. Einen Clou haben die SKSK architects noch bedacht: Das Prinzip von „Stecker" und „Dose" funktioniert nicht allein sinnbildlich: einige der Löcher sind an die Stromversorgung angeschlossen, so dass Leuchtelemente angeschlossen werden können.

La boutique Felissimo2 de Pekín tiene puntos verdes. Paredes y suelos están salpicados con 1.000 puntos que no son meros elementos decorativos. El concepto tieen su sistema: detrás de cada punto se esconde un agujero. A la toma correspondiente se pueden encajar todos los muebles o los objetos decorativos: percheros, barras, mesas, armarios o jarrones. De este modo, las posibilidades de presentar el producto son infinitas. A los arquitectos de SKSK se les ocurrió algo más: el principio del "enchufe" no solo funciona de forma simbólica, sino que algunos de los agujeros son verdaderas tomas a la red eléctrica, para así poder conectar los elementos luminosos.

La boutique de mode Felissimo2 à Pékin est couverte de pois verts. Plus de 1.000 points sont répartis sur les murs et le sol, mais ils servent plus qu'à la simple décoration. Tout le concept repose sur un système : un trou est caché derrière chacun des pois. Les connexions correspondantes sont attachées à tous les meubles et éléments de décoration : porte-manteaux, poteaux, tables, étagères et vases. Le résultat : toute une gamme de possibilités pour présenter les marchandises. Les architectes de SKSK proposent un autre éclairage : les principes de « connexions » et de « prises » ne sont pas seulement symboliques : certains des trous sont reliés au courant électrique pour que des éléments d'éclairage puissent y être insérés.

La boutique di moda Felissimo2 a Pechino è a pois verdi. Sulle pareti e sui pavimenti sono distribuiti fino a 1.000 punti che non servono solo per la decorazione. Il tutto ha un sistema: dietro a ogni punto si nasconde un buco. Le spine adatte sono installate su tutti i mobili e sugli elementi decorativi: attaccapanni, stecche, tavoli, armadi, vasi per i fiori. In questo modo si creano una moltitudine di possibilità per presentare la merce. Gli architetti della SKSK hanno pensato anche a un clou: Il principio di "spina" e "presa" funziona non soltanto dal punto di vista simbolico: alcuni buchi sono allacciati alla corrente elettrica in modo che vi possano essere attaccati degli elementi di illuminazione.

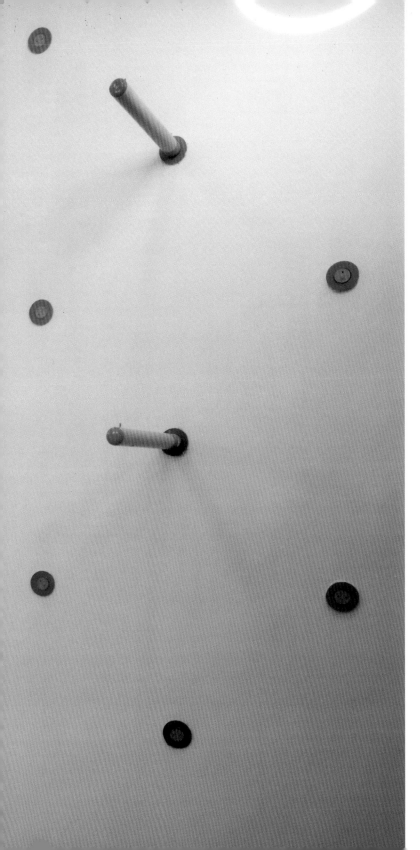

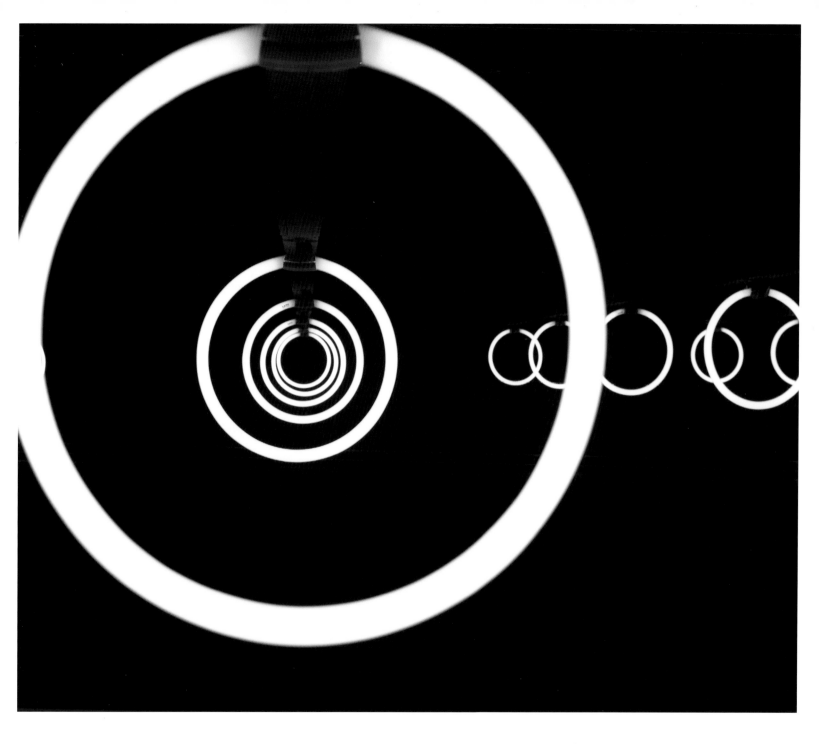

SKSK ARCHITECTS | BEIJING, CHINA

Website	www.sksk.cn
Project	Kid's Republic Bookstore
Location	Beijing, China
Year of Completion	2005
Building Materials	Furniture: MDF board, white oil paint finish partly covered with carpet; floor: artificial marble; ceiling: plasterboard, partly carpet
Color Specifications	Covers of children's picture books are very colorful, use of large quantity of multi-colored carpet to create a suitable space where picture books are collected, rainbow colors derived from the childhood memory of seeing beautiful rainbows.
Photo Credits	Minoru Iwasaki, Beijing

Introducing children to reading is simple in the Kid's Republic bookstore in Beijing. The SKSK architects know that children do not differentiate between playing and looking at or reading books. The planners have done their work in an intuitive and free manner. The result is a space for play and imagination. Events such as storytelling take place on the first level. A stairway leads to the book floor, accompanied by a rainbow band that winds through the room next to the stairs and constantly transforms itself: it becomes a bookshelf, a table, an archway, ceiling, and an armrest on the stairs. Children find a place to read in the round holes that are built into the bookshelves.

Kinder an das Lesen heranzuführen, ist in der Buchhandlung Kid's Republic in Peking einfach. Die SKSK architects wissen, dass Kinder nicht zwischen spielen und Bücher ansehen oder lesen trennen. Die Planer selbst haben sich intuitiv und frei an die „Arbeit" gemacht. Entstanden ist ein Raum für Spiel und Phantasie. In der ersten Ebene finden Events statt, wie Geschichten erzählen. Eine Treppe führt zu der Bücheretage, begleitet von einem Regenbogen-Band, das sich neben der Treppe durch den Raum windet und sich ständig verwandelt: Es wird zum Bücherregal, Tisch, Tor, Decke und zur Armlehne an der Treppe. Kinder finden Platz zum Lesen in runden Löchern, die in die Bücherregale eingelassen sind.

Acercar a los niños a la lectura es muy sencillo en la librería pekinesa Kid's Republic (República Infantil). Los arquitectos de SKSK son conscientes de que los niños no diferencian entre jugar y ver libros o leerlos. Los propios diseñadores se pusieron manos a la obra de manera intuitiva y libre. El resultado fue un espacio pensado para jugar y fantasear. En la primera planta se organizan lecturas de cuentos. A la planta de los libros se llega por una escalera, acompañada siempre por una franja en forma de arco iris que se extiende por toda la estancia y que se transforma sin cesar: en una estantería para libros, en una mesa, en una puerta, en el techo o en la barandilla de la escalera. Los niños pueden leer en unos orificios circulares practicados en las estanterías.

Initier les enfants à la lecture est simple à la librairie Kid's Republic de Pékin. Les architectes de SKSK savent que les enfants ne font pas la différence entre jouer et regarder ou lire des livres. Les concepteurs ont fait leur travail de manière intuitive et libre. Le résultat : un espace pour le jeu et l'imagination. Des manifestations comme des lectures d'histoires sont organisées au rez-de-chaussée. Un escalier mène à l'étage des livres, accompagné par une bande arc-en-ciel qui traverse la pièce près des escaliers et se transforme constamment : elle devient une bibliothèque, une table, une arcade, un plafond et un accoudoir sur les escaliers. Les enfants y trouvent un lieu pour lire dans les trous ronds intégrés dans les rayonnages.

Riuscire a far leggere i bambini non è un'impresa nella libreria Kid's Republic di Pechino. Gli architetti della SKSK sanno che i bambini non fanno distinzione tra giocare e guardare o leggere dei libri. I progettisti stessi si sono messi al "lavoro" in modo intuitivo e libero. Così è nata una sala per il gioco e la fantasia. Al primo livello hanno luogo degli eventi come il raccontare delle storie. Una scala porta al piano con i libri, accompagnata da un nastro-arcobaleno che si snoda attraverso la sala accanto alla scala e che si trasforma costantemente: diventa uno scaffale per libri, un tavolo, un portone, un soffitto e un bracciolo sulla scala. I bambini trovano un posto per leggere dentro a dei buchi rotondi che sono incassati negli scaffali per libri.

SKSK ARCHITECTS | BEIJING, CHINA

Website	www.sksk.cn
Project	Lattice in Beijing
Location	Beijing, China
Year of Completion	To be completed in 2007
Building Materials	Reinforced concrete
Color Specifications	Mirror-finish stainless steel (gold), cast iron (black). Gold is one of China's traditional colors—transforming traditional elements such as the lattice pattern and golden color into modern architecture
Photo Credits	Courtesy of SKSK architects, Beijing

Designers from Beijing, Tokyo, and New York met to design the individual commercial facilities for the complex in Sanlitun, a lively place for nightlife in the embassy quarter of Beijing. A colorful mixture of various approaches and visions come together here. For the façade, the SKSK architects selected a golden-yellow shade—a color based on tradition—and created a Chinese atmosphere with it. The planners provided the façade with reflecting, golden-yellow panels—in part with uneven surfaces so that the sunshine during the day influences the effects of the colors. Traditional patterns decorate the screens of cast steel that hang in front of the façade.

Für den Komplex in Sanlitun, einem beliebten Ausgehort im Botschaftsviertel von Peking, kamen Designer aus Peking, Tokio und New York zusammen, um die einzelnen kommerziellen Einrichtungen zu gestalten. Eine bunte Mischung von unterschiedlichen Ansätzen und Visionen treffen zusammen. Für die Fassade wählen die SKSK architects einen gelbgoldenen Ton – eine traditionsverbundene Farbe – und schaffen damit chinesische Atmosphäre. Die Planer versehen die Fassade mit reflektierenden, gelbgoldenen Paneelen, zum Teil mit unebenen Oberflächen, so dass die Sonneneinstrahlung über den Tag die Farbwirkung beeinflusst. Traditionelle Muster dekorieren die vor die Fassade gehängten Abschirmungen aus Gussstahl.

Diseñadores venidos de Pekín, Tokio y Nueva York se encargaron de diseñar cada una de las instalaciones del centro comercial Sanlitun, situado en la concurrida zona de embajadas de la capital china, lo que hizo converger una colorida mezcla de diferentes enfoques y propuestas. Los arquitectos de SKSK eligieron para la fachada un tono dorado, color con mucha tradición. De este modo consiguieron crear un ambiente chino. Los planificadores cubrieron la fachada con paneles dorados reflectantes, algunos de ellos de superficie irregular, para que la luz del día hiciera variar los efectos cromáticos. Unos motivos tradicionales decoran las pantallas de acero colado que cuelgan ante la fachada.

Des designers de Pékin, Tokyo et New York se sont alliés pour concevoir les différentes installations commerciales pour ce complexe de Sanlitun, le lieu des nuits animées dans le quartier des ambassades de Pékin. Un mélange coloré de différentes approches et visions s'y retrouve. Pour la façade, les architectes de SKSK ont choisi une teinte dorée – une couleur basée sur la tradition – pour créer une atmosphère chinoise. Les concepteurs ont doté la façade de panneaux dorés réfléchissants – certaines surfaces sont inégales pour que le soleil modifie les effets de la couleur pendant la journée. Des motifs traditionnels décorent les écrans d'acier moulé suspendus devant la façade.

Per il complesso a Sanlitun, un luogo amato per le escursioni nel quartiere delle ambasciate a Pechino, si sono riuniti designer provenienti da Pechino, Tokio e New York per progettare i singoli allestimenti commerciali. Si incontra una miscela variopinta di approcci e visioni differenti. Per la facciata gli architetti della SKSK hanno scelto un tono giallo-oro – un colore legato alla tradizione – e hanno così creato un'atmosfera cinese. I progettisti hanno fornito alla facciata dei pannelli riflettenti giallo-oro, in parte con superfici non piane, così che l'irradiamento solare influisce durante il giorno sull'effetto dei colori. Dei disegni tradizionali decorano la protezione in acciaio fuso della facciata.

SMC ALSOP | LONDON, UK
AMEC | WARRIGTON, UK

Website	www.smcalsop.com
	www.amec.com
Project	Blizard Building
Location	London, UK
Year of Completion	2005
Building Materials	Pods of fibre glass or fabric tensioned over a steel skeleton; Main pavilion: steel structure with structural glazing incorporating bespoke art panels
Color Specifications	Colored glass, fabrics, carpets, laminated painted timber and panels
Photo Credits	Roderick Coyne

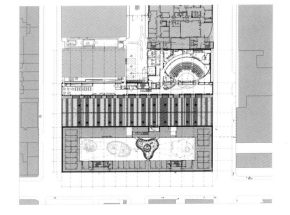

Research and theory meet at the Queen Mary medical school in London. On 97,000 sq. ft., the architects of SMC Alsop and Amec created a research space that interprets the theme of medicine in an imaginative manner. Pods that assume the communicative functions float in space. The "Mushroom Pod" acts as a reception area for visitors; the orange "Centre of the Cell" will house a multi-media science exhibition for local school children; the "Cloud Pod" and "Spiky Pod" contain meeting and seminar rooms. The bodies made of steel skeletons are covered with glass fiber and fabric on the outside. They are supported by steel pillars or suspended from them. The green "Lecture Theatre" offers space for up to 400 visitors.

Forschung und Lehre treffen in der medizinischen Hochschule Queen Mary in London aufeinander. Auf 9.000 m² lassen die Architekten von SMC Alsop und Amec einen Forschungsraum entstehen, der das Thema Medizin von phantasievoller Seite auffasst. Im Raum schweben „Hülsen" oder „pods", die kommunikative Funktionen wahrnehmen. Der „Mushroom Pod" am Boden dient als Empfangsbereich für Gäste; das orangefarbige „Centre of the Cell" wird eine wissenschaftliche Multi-Media Ausstellung für ortsansässige Schulkinder beherbergen; „Cloud Pod" und „Spiky Pod" beinhalten Räume für Meetings und Seminare. Die Körper aus Stahlskeletts, außen mit Glasfaser und Gewebe bespannt, werden von Stahlstützen getragen oder daran abgehängt. Das grüne „Lecture Theatre" bietet bis zu 400 Besuchern Platz.

La investigación y el estudio se unen en al Escuela Superior de Medicina Queen Mary de Londres. Sobre sus 9.000 m² erigieron los arquitectos de SMC Alsop y Amec un centro de investigación que aborda la medicina desde una perspectiva llena de fantasía. En él penden "vainas" que tienen una función comunicativa. La "vaina del hongo" a ras de suelo sirve de recibidor para las visitas; el "núcleo de la célula", de color naranja, acogerá una exposición científica multimedia para los escolares del lugar; la "nube" y la "vaina puntiaguda" comprenden salas para reuniones y seminarios. El armazón de acero está recubierto en su exterior con fibra de vidrio y textiles que se sujetan con puntales de acero o se cuelgan directamente al armazón. El "salón de conferencias", de verde, tiene un aforo para 400 personas.

La recherche et la théorie se rencontrent à l'école médicale Queen Mary de Londres. Sur 9.000 m², les architectes de SMC Alsop and Amec ont créé un espace de recherche qui interprète le thème de la médecine de manière imaginative. Des pods qui assurent les fonctions de communication flottent dans l'espace. Le « Pod Champignon » sert de zone de réception pour les visiteurs ; le « Centre de la Cellule », orange, abritera une exposition de science multimédia pour les enfants de l'école locale ; le « Pod Nuage » et le « Pod à Pointes » contiennent les salles de réunion et de séminaire. Les corps faits de squelettes d'acier sont couverts à l'extérieur de fibres de verre et de tissu. Ils sont soutenus par des piliers d'acier ou suspendus à eux. Le « Théâtre de Conférence » vert peut accueillir jusqu'à 400 visiteurs.

La ricerca e l'insegnamento si incontrano nella scuola superiore di medicina Queen Mary a Londra. Su 9.000 m² gli architetti della SMC Alsop e Amec hanno creato un locale per la ricerca che riprende il tema della medicina dal punto di vista della fantasia. Nell'ambiente sono sospesi degli "involucri" o dei "pods" che raccolgono le funzioni comunicative. Il "Mushroom Pod" sul pavimento serve come area di accoglienza per gli ospiti; l'arancione "Centre of the Cell" ospiterà una mostra scientifica multimediale per scolari del luogo; "Cloud Pod" e "Spiky Pod" contengono i locali per dei meeting e per dei seminari. I corpi dello scheletro in acciaio, rivestiti all'esterno con della fibra di vetro e del tessuto, vengono portati da sostegni in acciaio o vi sono attaccati. Il verde "Lecture Theatre" offre posto a 400 visitatori.

SPENGLER · WIESCHOLEK ARCHITEKTEN STADTPLANER | HAMBURG, GERMANY

Website	www.spengler-wiescolek.com
Project	Ensemble Pinnasberg, red + green between Reeperbahn and Habor
Location	Hamburg, Germany
Year of Completion	2004/2005
Building Materials	Pinnasberg 47: Façade in red enameled glass; Pinnasberg 45: Façade in printed enameled glass/folding shutters of steel as sun protection.
Color Specifications	Red, green
Photo Credits	Ralf Buscher, Hamburg, OPOLe6X6, Hamburg

Red and green meet in the ensemble at Pinnasberg between the red-light district on the Reeperbahn and Hamburg's harbor. The team of the Spengler Wiescholek Architekten unites two office buildings for different property developers. The façade of the northern head-end building of red enameled glass panels leans slightly outward and towers over the street area—glowing in red, the solitaire continues to be a prominent sign. Its southern partner behaves in a more reserved manner, as does its façade, which is also made of enameled glasses panels but printed with stylized ivy. The shiny surfaces mutually reflect each other and create an impression of lightness and spatial expansiveness.

Rot und Grün treffen in dem Ensemble am Pinnasberg zwischen dem Rotlichtviertel an der Reeperbahn und dem Hamburger Hafen zusammen. Das Team von den Spengler Wiescholek Architekten vereint zwei Bürogebäude für unterschiedliche Bauherren. Die Fassade des nördlichen Kopfbaus aus rot emaillierten Gläsern neigt sich leicht nach außen und stellt sich gegen den Straßenraum – rot leuchtend setzt der Solitär weithin ein markantes Zeichen. Zurückhaltend verhält sich sein südlicher Partner, dessen Fassade ebenso aus emaillierten, aber mit stilisiertem Efeu bedruckten Gläsern besteht. Die glänzenden Oberflächen spiegeln sich wechselseitig und erzeugen einen Eindruck von Leichtigkeit und räumlicher Weite.

Rojo y verde se combinan en este conjunto de la calle Pinnasberg de Hamburgo entre el barrio chino y el puerto. El equipo de arquitectos de Spengler Wiescholek unifica aquí dos edificios de oficinas para diferentes propietarios. La fachada norte, compuesta por cristaleras esmaltadas en rojo, se inclina ligeramente hacia el exterior invadiendo el espacio de la calle; desde lejos se distingue iluminada en rojo como todo un hito. La cara sur se muestra más reservada. Si bien la fachada está igualmente esmaltada, esta vez la conforman cristaleras con un estilizado estampado simulando la yedra. Las resplandecientes superficies producen reflejos y crean una sensación de liviandad y amplitud.

Le rouge et le vert se rencontrent dans l'ensemble de Pinnasberg entre le quartier rouge sur la Reeperbahn et le port d'Hambourg. L'équipe de Spengler Wiescholek Architekten a réuni deux bâtiments de bureaux pour différents promoteurs immobiliers. La façade du bâtiment de l'extrémité nord, en panneaux de verre rouge émaillé, penche légèrement vers l'extérieur et surplombe les rues - rouge brillant, le solitaire reste un signe proéminent. Son partenaire du sud se comporte de manière plus réservée, tout comme sa façade, également faite de panneaux de verre émaillé mais cette fois-ci imprimés de lierre stylisé. Les surfaces brillantes se reflètent mutuellement et créent une impression de luminosité et d'exubérance spatiale.

Rosso e verde si ritrovano in un insieme sul Pinnasberg tra il quartiere a luci rosse della Reeperbahn e il porto di Amburgo. La squadra degli architetti della Spengler Wiescholek unisce due edifici di uffici per differenti committenti di costruzioni. La facciata della costruzione frontale a nord fatta di vetri rossi smaltati si inclina leggermente verso l'esterno e si posiziona contro l'area stradale – in un rosso luminoso il solitario continua a rappresentare un segno marcante. Il suo partner a sud invece si comporta in modo più discreto, la sua facciata è anch'essa fatta di vetri smaltati, ma stampati con dell'edera stilizzata. Le superfici lucide si rispecchiano a vicenda e producono una impressione di leggerezza e di vastità di spazio.

STADTGUT ARCHITEKTEN | VIENNA, AUSTRIA

Website	www.stadtgut.com
Project	"let's have a ball" sportastic
Website	www.sportastic.at
Location	Feistritz/Drau, Austria
Year of Completion	2005
Building Materials	Steel frame construction with ventilated façade that has breathable plastic awnings
Color Specification	Orange plastic awning, orange India rubber
Photo Credits	Michael Nagl, STADTGUTarchitekten

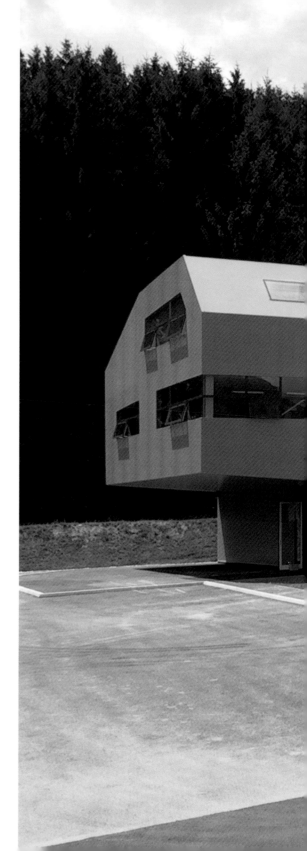

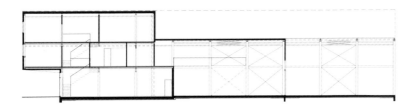

let's have a ball

SPORTASTIC

Seen from the autobahn, something is glowing on the green meadow. The manufacturer of sporting equipment, of balls and tennis rackets, was the first to set up office in the new business park in Feistritz/Drau. The building has been erected as a steel skeleton with insulated aluminum panels serving as the substructure for a breathing plane that provides a smooth surface without any gaps. The projection above the entrance area gives the building a sense of dynamics, which is intensified by the orange. The color of the company logo attains a new significance and transforms the company headquarters into a marketing instrument and the façade into an advertising media—corporate architecture at its best.

Von der Autobahn aus leuchtet es auf der grünen Wiese. Der Hersteller von Sportartikeln, von Bällen und Tennisrackets, lässt sich als erster auf dem neuen Betriebsansiedlungsgebiet in Feistritz/Drau nieder. Das Gebäude ist als Stahlskelett errichtet, gedämmte Alupaneele dienen als Unterkonstruktion für eine atmungsaktive Kunststoffplane, die für eine fugenlos glatte Oberfläche sorgt. Die Auskragung über dem Eingangsbereich verleiht dem Gebäude Dynamik, die das Orange verstärkt. Die Farbe des Firmenlogos erlangt eine neue Bedeutung und verwandelt den Firmensitz zum Marketing-Instrument und die Fassade in einen Werbeträger – Corporate Architecture pur.

Desde la autovía se distingue en medio de los verdes prados. El fabricante de artículos deportivos, pelotas y raquetas de tenis fue el primero en establecerse en las nuevas instalaciones de la empresa en Feistritz/Drau (Austria). La construcción cuenta con un armazón de acero; unos paneles de aluminio prensado le sirven de infraestructura a las lonas de material plástico transpirable que conforman una superficie lisa y hermética. El saledizo sobre la entrada aporta dinamismo al edificio, acrecentado por el color naranja. El color del logotipo de la empresa adquiere un nuevo significado y transforma su sede social en un instrumento de marketing y la fachada en un soporte publicitario: arquitectura corporativa en estado puro.

Vue depuis l'autobahn, quelque chose brille dans la verte prairie. Le fabricant d'équipement sportif, de balles et de raquettes de tennis a été le premier à mettre en place un bureau dans le nouveau parc commercial de Feistritz/Drau. Le bâtiment a été érigé comme un squelette d'acier avec un panneau d'aluminium isolé servant de sous-structure pour un plan aéré offrant une surface lisse, sans aucun trou. La projection au-dessus de l'entrée confère au bâtiment une sensation de dynamisme, intensifiée par la couleur orange. La couleur du logo de l'entreprise revêt une nouvelle signification et transforme le siège de la compagnie en instrument de marketing et la façade en média publicitaire – de l'architecture d'entreprise portée au plus haut niveau.

Dall'autostrada si vede una luce sul prato verde. Il produttore di articoli sportivi, di palle e racchette da tennis è stato il primo a insediarsi nella zona industriale di Freistritz/Drau. L'edificio è stato costruito come scheletro in acciaio, i pannelli isolanti servono da sottostruttura per un telone sintetico traspirante, che fa sì che ci sia una superficie liscia senza giunzioni. L'aggetto sulla zona ingresso conferisce all'edificio una dinamica che viene rafforzata dall'arancione. Il colore del logo della ditta acquisisce un nuovo significato e trasforma la sede dell'azienda in uno strumento di marketing e la facciata in un mezzo pubblicitario – puro Corporate Architecture.

UNSTUDIO | AMSTERDAM, NETHERLANDS

Website	www.unstudio.com
Project	Jewish Historical Museum
Website	www.jhm.nl
Location	Amsterdam, Netherlands
Year of Completion	2007
Building Materials	Wood, glass, multiplex, paint, LED lighting. Furnishings in cafe, ticket desk, cloakroom, auditorium and bookshop
Color Specification	Concept 'Colored White'; green, blue and yellow accents. (Yellow used for way finding and to brighten more enclosed walkways)
Photo Credits	Christian Richters, Münster

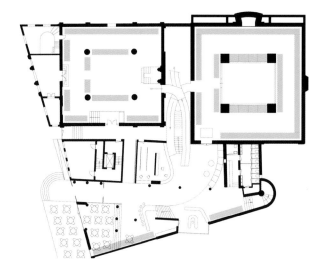

The museum in Amsterdam does not just see itself as a holocaust museum but shows the history of the Jews in the Netherlands, which began around 1600. With its events, the museum stands at the center of contemporary culture and the optimistic, self-confident Jewish way of life. The design by the UNStudio unifies the buildings of four synagogues under one roof. Each of the synagogues has an individual interior. The idea of a colored white means that a feeling of neutrality dominates throughout. But when chairs are moved or the doors of closets and toilets are opened, color appears and gives the room a character of its own at second glance.

Das Museum in Amsterdam versteht sich nicht als reines Holocaust-Museum, sondern es zeigt die Geschichte der Juden in den Niederlanden, die um 1600 beginnt. Mit seinen Veranstaltungen steht das Museum in der Mitte der zeitgenössischen Kultur und des optimistischen und selbstbewussten jüdischen Lebens. Der Entwurf des UNStudio vereint die Gebäude von vier Synagogen unter einem Dach. Die Synagogen erhalten jede ein individuelles Interieur. Die Idee von einem gefärbten Weiß bedeutet, dass überall ein Gefühl von Neutralität herrscht. Wenn aber etwa Stühle bewegt oder Türen von Schränken, Toiletten geöffnet werden, kommt Farbe zum Vorschein, die dem Raum auf den zweiten Blick einen eigenen Charakter verleiht.

No hay que entender este museo de Amsterdam como un museo dedicado al Holocausto, sino que muestra la historia de los judíos en Holanda, cuyo origen se sitúa en torno al 1600. Sus exhibiciones colocan al museo en el centro de la cultura contemporánea y del estilo de vida judío, optimista y confiado. El diseño de UNStudio aúna cuatro sinagogas bajo un mismo techo, cada una de las cuales con un interior individualizado. El blanco simboliza la idea del dominio absoluto de un sentimiento de neutralidad. Al mover una silla, la puerta de un armario o la de un aseo, aparecen los colores, otorgándole a este espacio un nuevo carácter.

Ce musée d'Amsterdam ne se voit pas uniquement comme un musée de l'holocauste mais expose toute l'histoire des Juifs aux Pays-Bas, histoire qui remonte aux environs de 1600. Avec ses expositions, le musée est le centre de la culture contemporaine et reflète le style de vie juif, optimiste et confiant. Le design des UNStudio unit les bâtiments de quatre synagogues sous le même toit. Chacune des synagogues a un intérieur différent. L'idée de blanc coloré signifie qu'un sentiment de neutralité domine partout. Mais quand les chaises sont déplacées ou que les portes des placards et des toilettes sont ouvertes, la couleur apparaît et donne un caractère particulier à chaque pièce en un clin d'œil.

Il museo di Amsterdam non si intende solamente come puro museo sull'olocausto, ma mostra la storia degli ebrei nei Paesi Bassi, storia che inizia intorno al 1600. Con le sue manifestazioni il museo si ritrova in mezzo alla cultura dell'epoca e della vita ebraica ottimista e sicura di sé. Il progetto del UNStudio unisce sotto un unico tetto gli edifici di quattro sinagoghe. Le sinagoghe contengono ognuna un interno individuale. L'idea di un bianco colorato significa che ovunque regna una sensazione di neutralità. Ma se vengono per esempio mosse delle sedie o aperte le porte degli armadi o dei bagni, appaiono dei colori che, guardando meglio, danno allo spazio un proprio carattere.

Mediatheek
Resource Centre

maandag - vrijdag
13 - 17 uur

Monday - Friday
1 - 5 pm

UNSTUDIO | AMSTERDAM, NETHERLANDS

Website	www.unstudio.com
Project	Agora Theatre
Location	Lelystad, Netherlands
Year of Completion	2007
Building Materials	Underlying structure of steel and concrete, skin of steel, glass and perforated aluminum façade of differently colored steel and perforated aluminum panels; foyer: ceiling from aluminum lamellae, full color wallpaper; theatre hall: walls with profiled acoustic and perforated panels, plasterboard panels, tufted polyamide carpet; pink painted ribbon
Color Specification	Varying shades of orange, based on setting sun. Yellow, small theatre; red, large theatre; pink, handrail foyer; blue, muiltifunctional rooms. These colors are also used for wayfinding in the building, by means of colored doors and LED lighting.
Photo Credits	Christian Richters, Münster

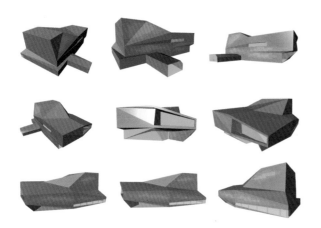

The evening sun above Lelystad inspired the UNStudio in its color scheme for the Agora Theater. The façade of the sculpture consists of steel and perforated aluminum panels that are partially layered. The yellow to orange shades of colors create a kaleidoscopic effect when the visitors walk around the building. In the foyer, pink stair balustrades move toward the light and astonish the eye: It searches for the customary wall surfaces and right angles in vain. The hall—the heart of the building—is where visitors watch theater or music performances. The "folded" walls assume one of the supporting roles and are responsible for the very good acoustics.

Die Abendsonne über Lelystad inspirierte das UNStudio zur Farbgebung des Agora Theaters. Die Fassade der Skulptur besteht aus Stahl- und perforierten Aluminiumpaneelen, die zum Teil geschichtet sind. Die gelben bis orangenen Farbschattierungen bewirken einen kaleidoskopischen Effekt, wenn der Besucher sich um das Gebäude bewegt. Im Foyer falten sich pinke Treppenbrüstungen dem Licht entgegen und erstaunen das Auge: Gewohnte ebene Wandflächen und rechte Winkel sucht es vergebens. Im Saal, dem Herz des Gebäudes, verweilen die Besucher, hier spielt das Theater oder die Musik. Die „gefalteten" Wände übernehmen eine der tragenden Rollen und zeichnen sich verantwortlich für die sehr gute Akustik.

El sol del atardecer en Lelystad sirvió de inspiración a UNStudio para elegir la paleta cromática del Teatro Agora. La fachada de esta construcción es de acero con paneles de aluminio perforado parcialmente recubierto. Las sombras amarillas y anaranjadas hacen que el visitante perciba un efecto caleidoscópico mientras bordea el edificio. En el vestíbulo, la balaustrada de peldaños rosas se dirige hacia la luz y llega a deslumbrar, por lo que la vista busca en vano planos convencionales y ángulos rectilíneos. En el auditorio – el corazón del edificio – se disfruta de la música o del teatro. Las paredes "plegadas" adquieren todo el protagonismo y son las responsables de la notable acústica.

Le soleil couchant au-dessus de Lelystad a inspiré à l'UNStudio son agencement de couleurs pour le Théâtre Agora. La façade de la sculpture consiste de panneaux d'acier et d'aluminium perforé partiellement superposés. Le camaïeu de jaune et d'orange crée un effet kaléidoscopique quand les visiteurs parcourent le bâtiment. Dans le foyer, les balustrades roses se déplacent vers la lumière et étonnent l'œil : il cherche en vain les surfaces murales habituelles et les angles droits. C'est dans le hall – le cœur du bâtiment – que les visiteurs assistent aux performances théâtrales ou musicales. Les murs « pliés » jouent les seconds rôles et sont responsables de l'excellente acoustique.

Il sole al tramonto su Lelystad ha ispirato il UNStudio a identificare il colore per il teatro Agora. La facciata della scultura è composta da pannelli in acciaio e in alluminio perforato, che sono in parte a più strati. Le sfumature che vanno dal giallo all'arancione creano un effetto caleidoscopico, quando il visitatore gira intorno all'edificio. Nell'atrio si snodano delle ringhiere rosa verso la luce e stupiscono l'occhio: che cerca invano delle superfici piane sulle pareti e degli angoli retti. I visitatori si trattengono nella sala, il cuore dell'edificio, dove si fa teatro o si suona la musica. Le pareti "ripiegate" rivestono un ruolo principale e sono responsabili per un'ottima acustica.

INDEX

© 2007 daab
cologne london new york

published and distributed worldwide by
daab gmbh
friesenstr. 50
d - 50670 köln

p + 49 - 221 - 913 927 0
f + 49 - 221 - 913 927 20

mail@daab-online.com
www.daab-online.com

publisher ralf daab
rdaab@daab-online.com

creative director feyyaz
mail@feyyaz.com

© 2007 edited and produced by fusion publishing gmbh stuttgart . los angeles
www.fusion-publishing.com

team
christiane niemann (editor, text), katharina feuer (editorial assistance, layout)
sabine henssen (text), alphagriese (translation)

photo credits
coverphoto courtesy of ag zimmermann + code unique, backcover christian richters, münster
introduction page 9 marc cramer, 11 thomas richter, 13 lukas roth, 15 johanna diehl; dominik jörg,
17 daigo ishii + future-scape architects

printed in china
www.everbest.eu

isbn 978-3-86654-005-7